A Word-Based Vision of Humanity
Transcending Violent Behaviours

PEACE
By Jesus Christ

Learning war no more

Rodney John Stephens

Peace By Jesus Christ - Learning war no more

ISBN 978-1-7638687-0-0

First edition printed 2025

Copyright © 2025

Rodney John Stephens

Cover Design:

COPMEDIA

Published by COPMEDIA

Sydney NSW Australia

COPMEDIA.COM.AU

COP
Media

Ephesians 4:3
Endeavouring to keep the unity
of the Spirit in the bond of
PEACE

Romans 15:33,
Now the God of Peace be with you all.
Amen.

Contents

John 16:33,
"These things I have spoken unto you,
that in me ye might have PEACE.
In the world ye shall have tribulation:
but be of good cheer;
I have overcome the world."

Preface

Introducing Peace as Heaven's Name

As we begin this journey through Peace by Jesus Christ: Learning War No More, it is essential to understand that Peace is not merely the absence of conflict, nor is it an abstract concept, a fleeting moment, emotion, place, or attitude. Peace is an endeavour, an experience, an encounter. Peace is a person. Jesus is our Peace because Jesus is Peace. Peace is the very essence of God's Kingdom. Peace is heaven's name, the defining characteristic of the divine order. Throughout the Scriptures, Peace is revealed as the foundation of God's will for humanity and creation. It is both the eternal destination of our spiritual journey, and the atmosphere in which we are called to live as followers of Christ, in the Spirit, Peace.

In this book, we will explore how Peace, in its fullest sense, is the identity of Jesus Christ and the central theme of His ministry. It is a divine gift, available to us now, and a promise of the future when His Kingdom of Peace will be fully established on Earth, as it is in Heaven. As you journey through these pages, you will come to see that Peace is more than something we pursue. Peace is the very presence of God manifested through His Son and brought into reality through His Spirit within and amongst us.

Jesus as Peace:
The Word Made Flesh

In John 1:14, we read that "And the Word was made flesh, and dwelt among us;" Jesus is the Word of God, and in Him, heaven's Peace took on human form. He is Peace incarnate, sent to bring reconciliation between humanity and God, as well as between neighbours and each and every person. His life, death, and resurrection are the ultimate revelation of God's desire for Peace on Earth.

Isaiah 9:6 proclaims Jesus as the Prince of Peace, and His teachings and actions demonstrate that He came to bring heaven's Peace to Earth. Throughout His ministry, Jesus modelled a life of forgiveness, reconciliation, and healing, inviting all who would listen to participate in the Kingdom of Peace that He was ushering in. His message is clear: the way to true Peace is found not in force or domination, but in the surrender to God's will and the practice of compassion and love toward one another, in the veracity of integrity to conscience.

Universal Call:
Live in Peace via the Golden Rule

At the heart of Jesus' teaching is the Golden Rule, found in Matthew 7:12: "Therefore all things whatsoever ye would that men should do to you, do ye even so to them." This is not just a moral guideline; it is the key to living in God's Peace. The Golden Rule invites us to transcend selfishness and violence, treating others with the same grace, kindness, and love that we ourselves desire. It reflects the very nature of God's Kingdom, a Kingdom where Peace reigns, and harmony is the rule, not the exception.

The Golden Rule is a universal principle, meant for all people in all times. It is a call to live out the Gospel of Peace in every aspect of life. E.g. in our relationships, groups, our communities, and even in our global interactions. As you will see throughout this book, adopting the Golden Rule for all is fundamental to embodying the Kingdom of Peace Jesus came to establish.

Scripture Spoken Before Written

The story of Peace did not begin when it was first written in the Scriptures, it began when God spoke it into existence. Genesis 1 tells us God spoke creation into being, and it was in that act of divine speech Peace was woven into the very fabric of existence. Long before it was written down, the Word of Peace was spoken by God, embodied in Jesus Christ, and revealed through the Holy Spirit.

This divine Word of Peace continues to speak into our lives today. It calls us to listen not only to what is written but to what the Spirit is speaking to our hearts, inviting us to participate in the unfolding of God's Peace on Earth. As we read the Scriptures, we must remember they are not just words on a page; they are living and active, calling us into communion with God and wholesome lives with one another.

Embracing the Gift of Peace on Earth

As we embark on this journey through Peace by Jesus Christ: Learning War No More, we are presented with an incredible opportunity, the opportunity to participate in the bringing of heaven's Peace to Earth. Jesus not only invites us to live in His Peace, but He also calls us to be ambassadors of that Peace, in a world that desperately needs it. Through our actions, words, and prayers, we can help to establish God's Kingdom of Peace in our homes, groups, tribes, communities, and even globally.

The Kingdom of Peace is not a distant dream; it is a present reality that we are called to live out every day. We can choose to be Peacemakers, to live according to the Golden Rule for all, to reject the world's ways of violence and conflict, and behold the way of Jesus Christ as His way of Peace.

This book is an invitation to enter into the fullness of God's Peace, to understand it not only as a personal blessing of miraculous Peace, but also as a divine calling. Together, let us embark on this journey to learn the ways of heaven's Peace, to leave behind the ways of war, and to embrace the better way Jesus has shown us, a way of Peace that transforms the world.

Introduction

The Word of Peace in a World of Conflict

In a world where conflict, violence, and war often dominate the headlines, the idea of Peace, true, lasting Peace, can feel distant and unattainable. Yet, the message of the Gospel and the life of Jesus Christ present a profound, transformative vision, that being, the possibility of learning war no more, and rather than training for war or domination, embracing an honest life governed by heaven's Peace instead. This is the vision this book seeks to explore, a word-based journey that invites us to transcend the violent behaviours and systems that have shaped human history so far and to enter into Jesus' Kingdom of Peace now and forevermore.

Peace by Jesus Christ is not just an ideal or a distant hope; it is a living reality, a divine invitation extended to each and every one of us to live in harmony with God, with one another, and with all creation. Jesus, who is Peace made flesh, embodies this reality, showing us that through faith, grace, and forgiveness, we can transcend the world's violent ways and become Peacemakers, honest people reflecting the Kingdom of Peace in our lives. Jesus in and amongst us bringing heaven to earth.

The Urgent Need for Transformation

Humanity has long been trapped in a cycle of violence and strife, with each generation inheriting the conflicts and issues of the past. From ancient wars to modern-day struggles, we have been conditioned to believe that force and superiority are the highways to Peace and harmony.

But this approach has only led to deeper divisions, more profound suffering, and an ever-present sense of fear.

At the heart of this problem is the philosophy of "Peace by superior firepower." The idea that might makes right and true Peace can only be secured through dominance. History has shown the failures of this mindset.

Violence has never brought lasting peace; it has only led to more violence, more brokenness, and more estrangement from the perfect will and way of God.

The world's systems have tried to bring about Peace through strength and power, but what the world needs, is not more of the same. Our world's need is transformation, a spiritual awakening, to the reality true Peace cannot be achieved through human strength or weapons.

It must come from God, through Jesus Christ, who came not to conquer through violence, force, or domination, but to bring reconciliation through sacrificial love.

This is why the message of Jesus as Peace is so urgent and relevant today. We have all seen the destruction war can bring to community, but Peace is not simply the absence of war; it is the presence of God's will on earth.

It is heaven's name and the very essence of His Kingdom. And it is through Jesus that His Peace has come into the world.

A Paradigm Shift from Violence to Education and Example

The Kingdom of God, as revealed by Jesus, offers a radical paradigm shift, mentoring and education replacing harm and punishment, a shifting from violence to Peace, from harm to help, from force to love, and from domination to grace and acceptance.

Jesus teaches us to embrace a new way of being, one that does not rely on violence, or fear, but is rooted in the truth of God's love for us, and the power of reconciliation to bring kindness into our world.

This shift is not just philosophical, it is deeply practical. In the Sermon on the Mount, Jesus provides us with a blueprint for living in God's Kingdom. He teaches us to turn the other cheek, to love our enemies, and to forgive seventy times seven, squared. These teachings are more than moral ideals, they are the foundation of a life lived in Peace, spiritually, personally, communally, and honestly.

The Gospel of Peace invites us to move beyond the retributive justice of the world's systems and to embrace God's restorative justice. Instead of retaliation, Jesus calls us to seek reunification. Instead of revenge, He offers us the power of forgiveness. This is the essence of learning to live without war, not merely in the sense of avoiding physical conflict, but in the sense of rejecting all forms of violence in our hearts, aggression in our relationships, and dominance in our communities.

Education and example are at the heart of this freedom and transformation. Jesus taught His disciples not by force, but by example, showing them the way of Peace through His own life, and death, His words, actions, and His teachings. As His followers, we are called to do the same, to educate others in the ways of Peace, to lead by example, and to embody the

Spirit of Peace in everything we do.

Cultivating Inner Peace:
The Work of the Holy Spirit

The journey toward Peace begins within. Jesus promised the Holy Spirit, the Comforter, His Peace, would come to guide us into all truth and kindness, including the truth of God's Peace. John 14:27 tells us Jesus gives us His Peace, not as the world gives, but as a divine gift that transcends all understanding.

This inner Peace or state of being is not dependent on external circumstances; it is the fruit of the Holy Spirit working in our hearts. As we learn to surrender to God's way, to trust in His goodness, and to follow the Spirit's leading, we cultivate an inner sense of calm, even in the face of adversity, keeping our peace, unity, and harmony. The Peace of Christ guards our hearts and minds, allowing us to respond to the world's challenges with grace, rather than with fear or anger. We can learn to rejoice and endeavour to keep the unity of the Spirit in the bond of His Peace.

This inner work of Peace is essential if we are to participate in the Kingdom of Peace Jesus came to establish and bring into being. Peace on earth begins with Peace in our hearts, our minds and conscience. It is the Spirit of God who makes this transformation possible.

A Spiritual Awakening
of a Greater Peace

As we journey through this book, you are invited into a spiritual awakening, an awakening to the greater reality of God's Peace. This is not the peace of the world, which is fragile and fleeting. It is a divine Peace that surpasses all understanding, a Peace that endures because it is a true blessing rooted in the eternal indwelling of God.

This awakening calls us to reimagine what Peace looks like in our own lives and in the world around us. It challenges us to lay down our weapons of war, whether physical, emotional, or spiritual, and to take up the armour of God, as described in Ephesians 6, an armour that equips us to stand firm in the face of adversity or conflict, not with violence or by strength of arms but in the power and wisdom the Gospel of Peace brings to bear.

The Kingdom of Peace is not just a future hope; it is a present reality we are called to live in every day. As we walk through the pages of this book, let us remain open to the Spirit's leading, allowing our hearts and minds to be transformed by the truth of God's Peace. Let us commit to learning war no more, to rejecting the world's ways of violence, and embrace the better way of Jesus Christ and His way of Peace. May His Peace be with you.

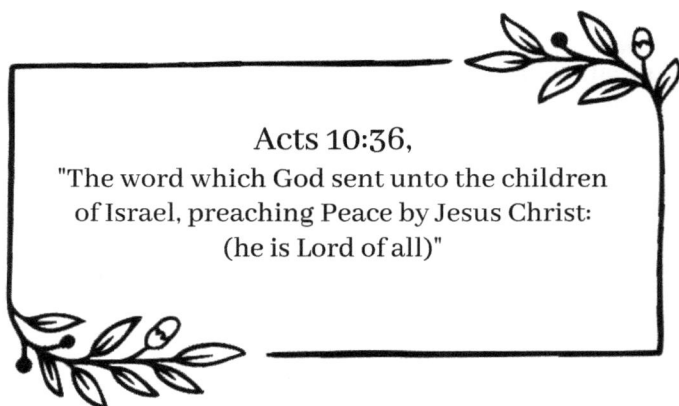

Acts 10:36,
"The word which God sent unto the children
of Israel, preaching Peace by Jesus Christ:
(he is Lord of all)"

Chapter 1

Jesus is Peace: Spirit and Kingdom of God.

Understanding Jesus as the Embodiment of Peace

From the beginning of creation, the Peace of God was the foundational state in which the universe was ordered and exists. Peace, in its truest form, is not merely the absence of turmoil or conflict, but the harmonious existence of all creation working together under God's sovereign reign. As error entered the world, this Peace was fractured. However, God's plan for restoration and reconciliation never wavered. The culmination of this divine plan is seen in the coming of Jesus Christ, who is not just a bringer of Peace but the embodiment of Peace itself.

Jesus is Peace. He represents God's kingdom on Earth, and His presence among humanity signifies the arrival of God's intended Peace for the world. Yet, this Peace was never meant to be understood merely as political tranquillity or the cessation of wars between nations. Instead, it is a spiritual reality, transcending the physical conflicts of this world and rooted in a deep, divine relationship with God and one another.

When Isaiah prophesied the coming of the Messiah, he declared that this Saviour would be the Prince of Peace (Isaiah 9:6). The Peace Jesus brings is not enforced by power or coercion but through grace, love, and self-sacrifice. The kingdom of God, which Jesus came to accomplish, is marked by this Peace, a Peace that the world, with all of its systems of control and domination, cannot understand, let alone see, or replicate.

This chapter seeks to lay the groundwork for understanding Jesus as the Spirit of Peace and the one who inaugurates the kingdom of God, a kingdom defined by love, humility, and rejoicing. In a world that often confuses power with peace, Jesus offers a radical departure, a Peace that heals relationships, reconciles humanity with God, and invites all of creation into a harmonious existence under God's sovereignty and will.

The Scriptural Foundations of Jesus as Perfect Peace

Throughout Scripture, the concept of Peace is intrinsically linked to the person and mission of Jesus. The Bible does not merely present Peace as a state of serenity or absence of war, but as an integral part of God's character, revealed through Jesus Christ. The Old Testament prophets foretold the coming of a Messiah who would establish an eternal reign of Peace. Isaiah 9:6-7 is a crucial passage that declares Jesus as the Prince of Peace, promising that His kingdom would be one of never-ending Peace, justice, and righteousness.

In the New Testament, this theme is developed further. Paul, in his letter to the Ephesians, explicitly states, "For He Himself is our Peace, who has made us both one and has broken down in His flesh the dividing wall of hostility" (Ephesians 2:14). Here, we see that Jesus' role as Peace-bearer extends beyond individuals to encompass all of humanity. By reconciling both Jews and Gentiles, breaking down barriers of hostility, and uniting them under His grace, Jesus brings the peace from Peace through His Peace into our divided world. This passage is crucial because it highlights how Jesus' Peace is not just personal but communal, He brings forward better for all. He mends relationships between different groups and calls all people into unity with His kingdom.

Similarly, in Colossians 1:19-20, we read, "For God was pleased to have all His fullness dwell in Him, and through Him to reconcile to Himself all things, whether things on earth or things in heaven, by making Peace through His blood, shed on the cross." The cross becomes the ultimate symbol of Peace, through Christ's sacrifice, Peace is achieved not by force but by self-giving love. The blood of Christ heals the rift between God and humanity and offers a path for all creation to be reconciled with its Creator.

How Jesus Brings Heaven's Peace to Earth

The kingdom of God that Jesus inaugurated is, at its centre, a kingdom of Peace. Throughout His ministry, Jesus made it clear His kingdom was not like the kingdoms of this world, which often rely on power, force, and domination to maintain order. John 18:36 reveals Jesus' words to Pilate: "My kingdom is not of this world. If it were, My servants would fight to prevent My arrest by the Jewish leaders. But now My kingdom is from another place." Jesus rejects the idea that Peace is established through strength of force; instead, He presents a kingdom built on servanthood, humility, the power of love and transformative energy kindness brings.

In the Beatitudes, Jesus teaches, "Blessed are the Peacemakers, for they will be called children of God" (Matthew 5:9). This verse offers a glimpse into the values of

God's kingdom: Peace is not passive; it is active. Peacemakers are those who go out into the world and work to re-unite others to God and each other, to be kind. They mirror the character of God and are recognized as His children because they carry the Spirit of Jesus, the ultimate Peacemaker.

One of the most profound acts for Peace Jesus performed was on the cross. Through His death and resurrection, He reconciled humanity with God. The cross is the ultimate symbol of Peace, because on it, Jesus conquered sin and death, not through violence but through sacrifice. Colossians 1:19-20 reveals through Christ, God reconciled all things to Himself, making Peace through the blood of His cross. This peace, in Peace, from Peace, goes beyond the personal, it is cosmic in scope, intended to heal the brokenness of all creation.

The kingdom of God, then, is not a distant futuristic ideal; it is a present reality for those who follow Christ and have Jesus within them. It is a kingdom where Peace reigns, where enemies become friends, where divisions are healed, help has victory over harm, and love triumphs over hatred. Luke 17:21 tells us that "the kingdom of God is within you," reminding us that we, as followers of Christ, are called to internalise His Peace and manifest the values of His kingdom in our daily lives. The Holy Spirit empowers us to live in harmony with each other and to become Peacemakers in our communities.

Living in the Reality of Jesus as Peace Today

As followers of Jesus, we are called to live in the reality of His Peace, (Colossians 3:15) allowing it to transform our hearts and minds, relationships, and communities. This peace from Peace is not something we achieve through our own efforts but is a gift from God, His Presence, given to us through the Holy Spirit. John 14:27 encapsulates this gift: "Peace I leave with you; My Peace I give to you. I do not give to you as the world gives. Do not let your hearts be troubled, and do not be afraid." We can remain at peace, in Peace, with His Peace.

The peace of Peace Jesus offers is distinct from the fleeting, conditional peace that the world tries to provide. The world's peace is often based in situation or on circumstance, if everything is going well, we feel at peace. But the Peace of Jesus is steady, enduring through the storms of life because it is fixed in a relationship with Him.

It is a Peace that "surpasses all understanding" (Philippians 4:7), guarding our hearts and minds in Christ Jesus, even when external circumstances are a total mess or in complete turmoil or disarray, still His miraculous peace remains.

To live in the reality of Jesus' peace of Peace today means allowing His Peace to guide our thoughts, actions, and relationships. It requires surrendering our desires for control and allowing the Holy Spirit to work in us, transforming our hearts to reflect the love and forgiving grace of Christ. It calls us to practice unity and forgiveness, to extend grace to everyone, everywhere, even when it is difficult.

One of the key ways we live out His Peace is by embracing the Golden Rule: "Do unto others as you would have them do unto you" (Matthew 7:12). This teaching, central to Jesus' message, is the foundation for living in Peace with others.

When we treat others with the same love, respect, and fairness that we desire for ourselves, we become instruments of God's Peace in the world.

Practical Applications:

Remaining in Peace:

Begin each day by intentionally reflecting on the blessing of miraculous Peace Jesus promises. Spend a few moments in prayer, asking the Holy Spirit to fill you with the Peace that surpasses all comprehension (Philippians 4:7). When challenges arise, pause, and remind yourself of Jesus' words in John 14:27: "Peace I leave with you, my Peace I give unto you: not as the world giveth, give I unto you. Let not your heart be troubled, neither let it be afraid." Take time to quiet your mind and allow His Peace to take root, reminding yourself that His Peace is not dependent on external circumstances, but on Christ's presence within you. Rejoice, our strength is in the joy of our Lord.

Living in Peace:

As followers of Christ, we are called to live out His Peace in our relationships and interactions with other people. This means actively choosing reconciliation over conflict, forgiveness over resentment, and love over retaliation. Consider your current relationships, where is there a need for Peace? Who do you need to forgive? Begin to practice the Peace of Christ by being a Peacemaker in your home life, workplace, groups, schools, and communities. Remember Ephesians 4:3, which encourages us to "make every effort to keep the unity of the Spirit through the bond of Peace."

Walking with His Peace:

Walking in Peace is a daily practice. It means letting go of control and trusting in God's plan, even when life feels uncertain or overwhelming. To walk with His Peace is to remain grounded in faith, even when the world around us feels chaotic and crumbling down. Reflect on Psalm 37:37, which says, "Mark the perfect, and behold the upright, for the be all of that person is Peace." As you go through your day, ask yourself how you can reflect Jesus' Peace to others. Whether in how you speak, listen, or act, strive to be an example of the kindness of Peace in every interaction.

Up Next

As we move into the next chapter, we will examine how history has tragically missed out on the Peace offered by Jesus. By choosing brute strength and force over reconciliation, humanity has often aligned itself with the philosophy of "peace by superior firepower," a mindset that has led to war, oppression, harm, and injustice. In Chapter 2, History Missing Heaven's Name, we will expose the consequences of a world that has overlooked the kingdom of Peace and what it means to reclaim that lost vision.

Recommended Bible Reading:

Mark 4:35-41 –Jesus Calms the Storm

This story demonstrates Jesus' authority over the physical and spiritual chaos, symbolising His role in bringing Peace into our lives.

Matthew 5-7 –The Sermon on the Mount: Blessed Are the Peacemakers

In these chapters, Jesus outlines the values of the kingdom of God, where Peace, humility, and love replace violence, pride, and hatred.

Group Study Questions

1. How does understanding Jesus as the embodiment of Peace challenge the world's common definitions of peace?
2. What role does reconciliation play in the Peace Jesus brings?
3. When does scripture first mention king of Peace?
4. In what ways does the Peace Jesus offers differ from the peace that the world offers?
5. How does the sermon on the mount affect you?
6. How do you see this contrast in your daily life?
7. Joke: What did Jesus say when he performed His first miracle? "Water ya waitin' for? Let's get this party started!

Chapter 2

History Missing Heaven's Name

A World Without Peace

From the dawn of civilization, humanity has strived for Peace. Yet, this pursuit has often been marked by violence, conflict, and might. From ancient empires to modern nations, the predominant philosophy of Peace has been "Peace by superior firepower." The belief that peace can only be achieved through supremacy, control, and force. This doctrine has shaped the course of history, leaving in its wake wars, conquests, devastation, tyranny, and oppression. So in this pursuit of peace, something crucial has been missing; the understanding true Peace is not achieved by power, but by the presence of Jesus Christ, the Prince of Peace.

History is filled with failed attempts to secure lasting peace through human effort alone. These attempts have overlooked a vital truth, without Jesus, who is the embodiment of Peace, humanity's vision of Peace is fundamentally flawed. In missing Peace as heaven's name, history has been shaped by a series of tragic missteps, where force was chosen over reconciliation, domination over forgiveness, and fear over love. This chapter exposes how history's failure to recognize and embrace Jesus' kingdom of Peace has led to a world defined by conflict rather than harmony.

The Philosophy of "Peace by Superior Firepower"

The idea of "Peace by superior firepower" is not a new concept. It has been the cornerstone of human empires and civilizations for millennia. From the Roman Empire's Pax Romana, which promised Peace through military dominance, to the modern era's arms races and nuclear deterrents, the belief has been that the best way to prevent war is to have the greatest capacity to wage it. This philosophy, while pragmatic in the eyes of many, is fundamentally flawed when viewed through the lens of Jesus' teachings.

The Roman Empire, often seen as a model of organized governance, achieved its "Peace" by subjugating peoples through violent conquest. The Pax-Romana, Roman Peace, was only sustained through brutal suppression of rebellion and the constant threat of force. It was a fragile Peace, one that depended on military might and coercion, not on justice, reconciliation, mutual respect, or benefit.

In the Old Testament, we see examples of this same principle at play. Kings like Pharaoh or Nebuchadnezzar maintained their empires through overwhelming force. Pharaoh's Egypt was built on the backs of enslaved peoples, and when Moses came to deliver the Israelites, Pharaoh's refusal to release his captives led to his downfall. The plagues of Egypt, culminating in the parting of the Red Sea (Exodus 14), reveal the futility of relying on human power to maintain Peace.

This philosophy persists in modern history. The World Wars of the 20th century were fought with the promise victory would bring lasting peace, yet they only gave rise to the Cold War, an era defined by an arms race where Peace was maintained through the threat of mutual destruction. Nations stockpiled weapons, each believing that only by having the most destructive arsenal could they prevent conflict. This doctrine of deterrence or holding back war by instilling fear of retaliation missed the fundamental truth. Peace is not born out of fear, but from love and mateship, assured, determined reconciliation.

Jesus, by contrast, rejected the notion of dominance. His Peace was not one of supremacy, but of humility and servanthood. In Matthew 5:39, Jesus teaches, "But I tell you, do not resist an evil person. If anyone slaps you on the right cheek, turn to them the other cheek as well." Jesus did not seek to overcome His enemies through violence, but through the radical love that confounds the world's logic. By turning the other cheek, Jesus invites us into a different way, a way that does not respond to force with force but seeks to overcome evil with good (Romans 12:21).

A Void Left in the Absence of Jesus' Kingdom of Peace

When history overlooks Jesus and His kingdom of Peace, it creates a vacuum, and that vacuum is often filled by violence, fear, and division. The absence of Jesus' Peace leaves humanity to its own devices, leading to fractured relationships between individuals, families, communities, and nations. The absence of Heaven's name, the name of Peace, has robbed us of a belief in Peace, which has led to a world still willing to go to war, where conflict is the norm and reconciliation is the exception.

Consider the long history of religious wars. While religion is meant to connect humanity with the divine and with each other, history shows religion has often been co-opted to justify violence and cruelty. The Crusades or Inquisitions, for instance, were wars fought in the name of God but were marked by bloodshed and conquest rather than the Peace and reconciliation that Jesus preached. The name of Peace was absent, replaced by the desire for power and control over people, sacred sites, doctrines, and brands. Without Peace being central to truth, humanity filled the void, believing in violence instead of Peace. For our beliefs determine our behaviour, what we believe to be true determines what we will do.

Even within the Church, there have been times when the pursuit of Peace has been overshadowed by division and hostility. The Protestant Reformation, while a necessary call for reform within the Church, led to centuries of sectarian violence between Catholics and Protestants. The wars and persecutions that followed were a direct result of humanity's failure to live in the Peace that Jesus offered. Instead of seeking unity and reconciliation in the body of Christ, many sought to impose their beliefs through force, missing the opportunity to reflect the Peace of Heaven by replacing Peace with their own brands.

When the Peace of Jesus is absent, societies fall into patterns of retribution rather than restoration. Justice is often equated with punishment, and systems of oppression take root. In many societies, women, and children, the vulnerable and the marginalised, have borne the brunt of violence. Without the Peace of Jesus guiding societal structures, violence becomes systemic, ingrained in laws, traditions, institutions, and culture. The structural violence against women and children is a glaring example of how history has missed Heaven's name and the consequences of it. Instead of providing protection and care for the vulnerable, societies have often perpetuated harm, using violence as a tool of control.

The Consequences of a World That Trusts in Violence

The consequences of a world that trusts in violence are evident in the cycles of war, poverty, and injustice that plague human history. When nations and individuals place their trust in force, trust the gun more than God, the result is often far from Peace but rather an escalation of damage and conflict. Violence begets violence, and the wounds of war and oppression leave deep scars on the human soul.

The 20th century is a prime example of the devastating effects of trusting in violence. World War I, often called "The Great War," was supposed to be the war that ended all wars. But it set the stage for World War II, a conflict even more destructive. The aftermath of these wars left much of the world in ruins, both physically and spiritually. Millions of lives were lost, and entire generations were marked by trauma and grief. The trust in violence as a means to achieve peace only led to more destruction.

The Cold War, which followed the world wars, was another manifestation of this misplaced trust. For decades, the world lived under the shadow of nuclear annihilation, as the superpowers stockpiled weapons capable of wiping out humanity several times over. This was not Peace, but a tense and fragile truce maintained through fear.

But these consequences are not limited to global conflicts. In personal relationships, communities, and nations, the absence of Jesus' Peace leads to brokenness. Families torn apart by conflict and lack of empathy and understanding, patience and grace, communities divided by prejudice and self-centredness, and nations fractured by civil unrest and division. All of these are the fruit of trusting in violence rather than the Peace that comes through the forgiveness and grace of Christ.

Jesus offers a different way. His Peace does not depend on

human strength but on divine love. In John 16:33, Jesus tells His disciples, "I have told you these things, so that in Me you may have Peace. In this world, you will have strife. But take heart! Rejoice, I have overcome the world." Jesus acknowledges that the world is full of trouble, yet He offers a Peace that transcends the conflicts and struggles of this life. His Peace is not the absence of strife, but the presence of God in the midst of it.

The Golden Rule as the Key to Peace

At the heart of Jesus' teachings on Peace is the Golden Rule for all: "Do unto others as you would have them do unto you" (Matthew 7:12). This simple yet profound command is the key to building a world culture of Peace. The Golden Rule for all challenges the philosophy of peace by superior firepower and force by calling for empathy, compassion, and mutual respect. It invites us to consider the needs and desires of others and to act in ways that promote their well-being, just as we would want them to fairly act toward us.

The Golden Rule for all turns the concept of Peace by strength on its head. Instead of seeking to dominate or control others to achieve Peace, Jesus calls us to serve and love one another, and to be kind. This is the essence of His kingdom, a kingdom where Peace is not enforced by power but flows naturally from relationships built on love, respect, and kindness. We gain Peace in friendship rather than frightening. When individuals and nations live by the Golden Rule for all, conflicts are resolved through empathy, dialogue and understanding, not through violence and force.

Living by the Golden Rule requires humility and a willingness to prioritise the needs of others. It is the practical outworking of Jesus' command to "love your neighbour as yourself" (Matthew 22:39). When we love our neighbours, whether they are close friends or distant enemies, we reflect the Peace of Jesus in our actions and we can live being kind and generous of Spirit.

Summary:

As we close this chapter, we have seen how history, in missing the name of Jesus' kingdom as Peace, has led to a world believing and placing faith in violence, oppression, and division. The philosophy of "Peace by superior firepower" has dominated human history, but it is a flawed and temporary solution that often escalates conflict rather than resolving it. In contrast, the Peace of Jesus offers a radical alternative to control by force. Jesus offers His Peace based on restoration, reconciliation, humility, grace, and love.

In Chapter 3: Reclaiming Our Conscience for Peace, we will explore how the ego and self-centredness capture our conscience, driving us toward conflict rather than Peace. We will examine how Jesus calls us to turn away from fear, force, and retribution, and to embrace reconciliation and the transformation of our conscience by aligning with the Spirit of God's kingdom of Peace. This next chapter will delve deeper into the inner transformation required for us to become agents of Peace in a troubled world.

Practical Applications:
Remaining in Peace:

To remain in Peace, we must guard our hearts against the temptation to respond to conflict with aggression or fear. Instead, we can take refuge in the Peace that Jesus offers, trusting that His presence will guide us through turbulent times. When faced with challenges, reflect on John 16:33: "In this world you will have trouble. But take heart and fear not for I have overcome the world!" Pray for God's Peace to fill your heart, and actively choose to remain calm in the face of adversity.

Living in Peace:

Living in Peace means applying the Golden Rule in our daily interactions. Practically, this could mean resolving disputes without resorting to harsh words or retaliatory actions. It also means being an advocate for those who are vulnerable, standing up against injustice and promoting reconciliation where divisions exist. Consider how you can live in the understanding of Romans 12:18: "If it is at all possible, as far as it depends on you, live at Peace with everyone."

Walking with His Peace:

Walking with the Peace of Jesus means carrying His Peace into every part of your life, into your relationships, your workplaces, schools, and your community. Ask yourself each day: "How can I reflect the Peace of Jesus in my actions today?" Whether through learning something new, simple acts of kindness, offering forgiveness, standing up for justice, strive to walk as an ambassador of God's Peace in a world that desperately needs to see it to believe it.

Group Study Questions

1. How has the philosophy of "Peace by superior firepower" influenced the course of history, and how does it differ from the Peace Jesus offers?
2. What are the consequences of a world that trusts in violence rather than in Jesus' kingdom of Peace?
3. How does the Golden Rule challenge the world's understanding of peace and offer a practical framework for living in harmony with others?
4. How does a peace by superior firepower impact modern life?

5. How has the absence of Jesus' Peace impacted vulnerable populations, such as women and children, throughout history?

❧⟫⟫⟫-⟨⟨⟨⟨❧

Recommended Bible Reading:
Exodus 7-14 −The Exodus and the Plagues of Egypt

This story highlights how Pharaoh's reliance on force and oppression ultimately led to his downfall and the liberation of the Israelites. It emphasizes that power and violence cannot bring lasting Peace.

Mark 16:15-17 −Commission to proclaim the Gospel to all the world.

In these verses Jesus commissions His disciples to go into all the world and proclaim the gospel to all creation.

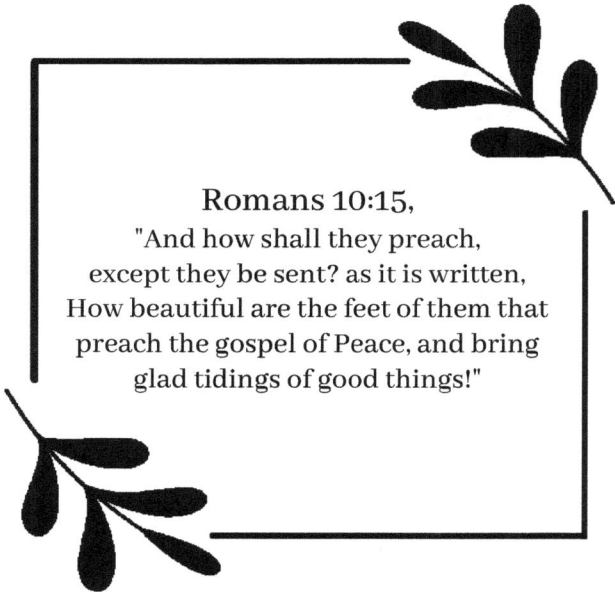

Romans 10:15,
"And how shall they preach,
except they be sent? as it is written,
How beautiful are the feet of them that
preach the gospel of Peace, and bring
glad tidings of good things!"

Chapter 3

Reclaiming Our Conscience for Peace

Conscience vs. Self Ego
- The Inner Conflict

At the core of every human being lies a conflict between the conscience and the ego. The conscience, guided by God's Spirit, calls us toward honesty, harmony, and kindness, while the ego/self is driven by self-interest, fear, self-preservation, and the desire for superiority which often leads us into chaos or conflict. This inner battle is the source of much of the violence, division, and unrest in the world today. As long as the ego dominates our thoughts and thus our actions, we remain trapped in cycles of self-righteousness, judgment, and strife.

Jesus calls us to an entirely different way of life, a life where the conscience is reclaimed and renewed through His Peace, the Spirit of God. In doing so, we are invited to step away from the need to be right and the temptation to fight for our own self-interest. Instead, we become agents of reconciliation, embodying the Peace of Christ within ourselves, in our relationships, groups, communities, and the world at large. Reclaiming our conscience means rejecting the destructive influence of the ego and embracing the transformative power of Jesus' grace and Peace, His love He has for us all.

This chapter will explore how the ego/self captures our conscience and drives us toward discord, and how Jesus' message of reconciliation offers a pathway back toward reclaiming our conscience for Peace. By turning back to God's Peace through grace and truth, we can break free from the grip of the ego/self and live as Peacemakers in a troubled world.

The Ego: Captivator of the Conscience

The ego or the part of us that seeks to preserve our own identity and way, highlight our own glory, and demand control, often captures the conscience, blinding us to the call of God's Peace and way. When the ego reigns, it leads us to seek dominance over others, to justify our actions regardless of harming others, and to defend ourselves at all costs. The ego demands to be right, thrives on pride, seeks to instil fear, tells us lies and is one of the greatest enemies of Peace. Some may say the devil is our ego.

In moments of conflict, the ego persuades us to see others as threats. We believe that in order to protect ourselves, we must attack, criticise, or undermine those who challenge us. This is evident not only in personal relationships, but in larger societal structures. Political disputes, wars, and social injustices are all manifestations of the ego-driven desire for control, superiority, self-emphasis, and interest. The ego/self convinces us that in order to be safe or significant, we must elevate ourselves at the expense of others.

Self-righteousness, a key characteristic of the ego, is a root cause of violence and conflict. When we believe we are unequivocally right, we leave no room for grace, dialogue, or understanding. We only fight when we believe we're right. This creates an atmosphere where judgment flourishes, and compassion is stifled. Matthew 7:1-5 speaks to this: "Do not judge, or you too will be judged. For in the same way you judge others, you will be judged, and with the measure you use, it will be measured to you." Jesus highlights how self-righteous judgment only serves to blind us further from seeing our own faults, and it prevents reconciliation or reconnecting.

The ego often distorts our understanding of justice, leading us to seek retribution, rather than restoration. When someone wrongs us, our ego demands punishment or revenge, believing that Peace can only be restored once justice has been served in our favour. But this is a false assumption of Peace, one built on vengeance rather than healing. True Peace, as Jesus shows, comes not from retribution, but from forgiveness and reconciliation. Romans 12:19 reminds us, "Do not take revenge, my dear friends, but leave room for God's wrath, for it is written: 'It is mine to avenge; I will repay,' says the Lord." What goes around comes around and it may take some time and patience to be fully accomplished.

Jesus: The Way to Reclaiming Our Conscience

Jesus invites us to a new way of life, one in which our conscience is liberated from the grasp of the ego and restored to its rightful place as the guide to our honesty, integrity, authenticity, our success, our moral compass, and voice in our spiritual life. Jesus' message of Peace is not just about avoiding conflict but about transforming our hearts and minds so that we can be born again agents of His kingdom of Peace, and Spirit, here on Earth. (John 3:5-7) To reclaim our conscience, we must first recognize the ways in which our ego/self has led us astray and surrender those parts of ourselves to God. We can ask Jesus to be our conscience for us and learn to trust His inner small voice all the more.

One of the key aspects of Jesus' teaching on Peace is the call to reconciliation. In Matthew 5:23-24, Jesus instructs us, "Therefore, if you are offering your gift at the altar, and there, remember that your brother or sister has something against you, leave your gift there in front of the altar. First, go and be reconciled to them; then come back and offer your gift to God." This passage underscores the importance of relationship and connection in the life of faith. Before we can truly worship God, we must seek to heal our broken relationships with others.

Reclaiming our conscience for Peace means that we no longer view others through the lens of competition, fear, or judgment. Instead, we see them as fellow image-bearers of God, worthy of love, respect, kindness, and grace. When we embrace this perspective, our interactions with others become opportunities for healing rather than strife. We move from being people who demand justice for ourselves to people who offer grace to others.

Jesus demonstrated this throughout His ministry. Whether He was healing the sick, forgiving sin, or calling for the outcasts of society to be embraced, Jesus consistently showed us the path to Peace is through love, and not condemnation. Luke 7:47-48 records Jesus' words to the sinful woman: "Therefore, I tell you, her many sins have been forgiven, as her great love shows. But whoever has been forgiven little, loves little." Jesus links forgiveness with love and Peace, demonstrating forgiveness sets both the giver and the receiver free, allowing true Peace to flourish.

The Role of Fear, Force, and Retribution in War

Fear is often the driving force behind conflict and war. Nations, communities, and individuals go to great lengths to protect themselves from perceived threats, even if it means harming others in the process. This fear-driven response is founded in the belief that our survival and success depend on our ability to clearly dominate or defend ourselves against others. The ego thrives on fear, convincing us that Peace can only be achieved through force, aggression, or control.

History is littered with examples of fear leading to violence. From ancient wars to modern conflicts, leaders and nations have justified acts of violence by claiming they were necessary to protect their people or ensure their nation's security.

Yet, as we have seen throughout the course of history and civilisation, violence only breeds more violence. World War I, for example, was believed to be the "war to end all wars." But instead, it laid the foundation for World War II and the ongoing cycle of violence that has plagued the 20th and 21st centuries. Abusers go on to abuse, unless the cycle is disrupted by new and better truths.

Retribution, like fear, is another force fuelling war and conflict. The desire for revenge, whether at a personal or national level, perpetuates these cycles of abuse and violence. Romans 12:17 warns against a mindset of repaying anyone evil for evil. Be careful to do what is best for all, in the eyes of everyone, repay evil with good. Jesus teaches us that true justice is not found in getting even, but in showing grace, having mercy, and seeking reconciliation.

When fear and retribution dominate, Peace is almost impossible. However, Jesus offers us a different path, a path where fear is replaced by faith trusting in God's provision and protection, and retribution is replaced by forgiveness and grace.

In Matthew 5:9, Jesus declares, "Blessed are the Peacemakers, for they will be called children of God." Peacemaking is the act of stepping away from fear, revenge and retribution and instead choosing to trust in God's plan for Peace and restoration, we choose faith over fear and place our trust in God more than in the gun.

Turning Back to God's Peace Through Reconciliation

Reclaiming our conscience for Peace means turning away from the ego's demands for self-importance and turning back to God's invitation to reconcile and be at one in His Peace. Reconciliation is at the heart of the Gospel message, it is the process by which we are brought back into a better relationship with God, and it is His model for how we are to engage with others.

Jesus' ministry was focused on reconciliation and bringing people back into a relationship with God and with each other. In 2 Corinthians 5:18-19, Paul writes, "All this is from God, who reconciled us to Himself through Christ and gave unto us the ministry of His reconciliation: that God was reconciling the world to Himself in Christ, not counting people's sin against them." As followers of Jesus Christ, we are called to participate in this ministry of reconciliation. This means actively seeking to heal relationships, mend divisions, and promote Peace in our communities. We can learn to remain at peace, in Peace, with His Peace.

Reconciliation is not easy. It requires vulnerability, humility, and a willingness to acknowledge our own faults. It also requires forgiveness, which is often the most challenging part of the process. But when we embrace reconciliation, we reflect the heart of God and become instruments of His love, His Peace, grace, kindness, and truth.

The Call to Live as Agents of Peace in a Troubled World

The world is full of troublemakers and in desperate need of Peacemakers, those who are willing to stand in the gap between right and wrong, conflict and reconciliation, between division and unity. (Matthew 9:37) As followers of Christ, we are called to be agents of Peace, bringing the message of Peace and goodwill to a world fractured by conflict and troublemakers. This calling is not passive; it is an active, daily pursuit of justice, grace, and healing. Romans 12:18 says, "If it is possible, as far as it depends on you, live at Peace with all." While Peace may not always be immediately attainable in every situation, we are called to do everything within our power to foster it, making reconciliation a priority over retribution.

Living as agents of Peace means engaging with the world's brokenness rather than retreating from it. We must address societal structures that perpetuate violence, inequality, and division. Jesus' Peace does not ignore injustice but seeks to dismantle the systems that create and sustain it. This may involve advocating for the oppressed, standing up for those without a voice, powerless, and working to transform communities into places where Peace and justice prevail.

The Holy Spirit empowers us to carry out this mission.

We are not left alone to achieve Peace by our own strength or means. His Spirit works in us and through us, guiding us in moments of struggle, giving us the courage to seek reconnection, and equipping us to be Peacemakers in our families, workplaces, societies, and nations. Galatians 5:22 reminds us that Peace is a fruit of the Spirit, cultivated through a life lived in submission to God's will.

Summary:

In this chapter, we have explored how reclaiming our conscience for Peace involves turning away from the ego/self and its demands and embracing the Peace of Jesus through reconciliation and grace. This journey is not without challenges, but it is the path that leads to true and everlasting Peace, both within ourselves and in our relationships with others.

In Chapter 4: The Better Tree: A Path to Continuous Growth and Peace, we will examine how choosing the path of continuous improvement, grace, and unity over judgment and condemnation leads us on into a deeper experience of God's Peace. We will explore how the Holy Spirit plays a vital role in our growth as individuals and communities, and also how rejecting judgment allows us to experience lasting Peace.

Group Study Questions

1. How does the ego/self capture our conscience and lead us away from the Peace of Christ?
2. What role does fear play in perpetuating conflict, and how can we overcome it through Jesus' teachings?
3. In what ways does reconciliation, both with God and with others, restore Peace in our lives and communities?
4. How can we live as agents of Peace in a world that often prioritises retribution over reconciliation?
5. Joke: What does Jesus smell like? Heaven Scent.

Practical Applications:

Remaining in Peace:

Remaining in Peace requires a conscious effort to align our hearts and minds with Christ's teachings. Take time each day to reflect on areas where your ego might be leading you away from Peace. Pray for the strength to surrender your ego/self to God and ask the Holy Spirit to fill your heart with Christ's Peace. Reflect on Romans 12:19, reminding yourself that God is the ultimate judge, and it is not your role to seek revenge or dominate others.

Living in Peace:

Living in Peace involves taking active steps to promote grace in your connections and relationships. Is there someone you need to forgive or ask for forgiveness from? Initiate conversations that may be difficult but are necessary for healing and restoration. Practice humility by listening to others' perspectives and acknowledging your own shortcomings. By living out the principles of reconciliation, you bring Peace to your relationships and reflect Christ's kingdom here on earth.

Walking with His Peace:

To walk with His Peace means allowing the Peace of Christ to guide your actions, even in moments of turmoil or uncertainty. When faced with challenges, seek guidance from the Holy Spirit on how to respond with grace rather than defensiveness. Walking in Peace is a daily commitment to choose love over fear, unity over division, and humility over pride. Reflect on Proverbs 3:17; Her ways are ways of pleasantness, and all her paths are Peace. As a child of God, carry His Peace into every area of your life, trusting His Spirit will lead you along wisdom's path of Peace.

Recommended Bible Reading:
Luke 15:11-32 –The Prodigal Son's Reconciliation

This parable demonstrates the power of forgiveness and reconciliation, both between the father and the prodigal son, and within the family. It shows the path to Peace through grace and restoration.

Genesis 45:1-15 –Joseph Forgives His Brothers

In this story, Joseph, after enduring betrayal and hardship, chooses to forgive his brothers, offering forgiveness brings Peace to his family and serves as an example of overcoming conflict with love.

Colossians 1:9-23 –Welcome to Peace

Through Christ, we are delivered from darkness and brought into His Kingdom of Peace. Jesus, the image of God, reconciles all through His blood. In Him, we stand firm, growing in wisdom and strength. Grateful, this is our welcome, peace through His cross, hope in His gospel, and life everlasting.

Colossians 2:8-23 –Warning of false doctrine

Beware of deception, philosophies, and traditions of men that are not of Christ. In Him dwells all fullness, and we are complete in Him. The cross triumphs over every power. Why follow human rules like touch not and taste not when Christ has freed us? Mere commands of men have no true value. Hold fast to Jesus, not shadows but the substance, life in Him alone.

Chapter 4

A Path to Continuous Growth and Peace

Choosing the Better Tree Over the Tree of Judgment

In the Garden of Eden, are two trees representing two schools of thought. Because of the work of Jesus, humanity is now given a choice to eat from the Tree of Life or continue munching on the Tree of Knowledge of Good and Evil. The Tree of Life symbolizes growth, unity, and Peace, a continuous relationship with God that fosters life in its fullest form.

The Tree of Knowledge of Good and Evil, however, represents judgment, division, and separation from God. When Adam and Eve chose to eat of the latter after instructed not to, they ushered in an era where human beings became preoccupied with judgment and distinguishing right from wrong, but without the divine grace that brings healing and Peace.

This story is not just about a choice made in the distant past; it reflects a choice we face daily. Will we choose the better tree? The path of continuous growth, never ending Peace, and connection with God, as we aim for better, or will we live in the shadow of the tree of judgment, where division, strife, and conflict reign? The path of the better tree is a path of Peace, one that calls us to reject standing in judgement of right from wrong and embrace the Spirit of grace, truth, and unity and ask what's better instead.

In this chapter, we explore how choosing the better tree leads us to better ways to live in harmony with one another, fostering continuous spiritual growth and Peace in our communities. We will discuss how living in the Spirit of Christ, the true Tree of Life, guides us toward rejecting judgment and pursuing restoration of things through grace, and growth in new truths.

The Tree of Judgment: How It Divides and Destroys

The Tree of Knowledge of Good and Evil represents humanity's desire to determine right from wrong on our own terms, in our own eyes, and without God's wisdom. This is at the heart of self-righteousness, in our own eyes from our own viewpoint, a condition that leads to judgment, division, and conflict, because what is right for you might not be right for others. In the story of Adam and Eve, the moment they ate from the tree of knowledge, their eyes were opened to right from wrong, becoming vainly God-like, not to Peace, life or understanding, but instead, to closed-mindedness, selfishness, death, and deception. They became aware of their own nakedness and immediately felt shame. This shame, paired with the impulse to judge, led to separation from God and from each other.

When we rely on judgment rather than grace, we create barriers between ourselves, God, and others. Judgment fosters an environment of exclusion, where those who fail to meet certain standards or criteria, are cast out, ostracized, criticized, or marginalized. This is evident in many aspects of society, from family power dynamics to global political systems. When we live under the shadow of judgment, condemnation, and finger pointing, we can lose sight of our shared humanity and common calling to love and support one another.

Luke 6:37 echoes this truth, with Jesus' teaching, "Do not judge, and you will not be judged. Do not condemn, and you will not be condemned. Forgive, and you will be forgiven." Jesus wants us to reject the impulse to judge other people and instead extend forgiveness, grace, and patience, all the while gaining understanding, through empathy, care and listening. (Mark 12:29) Living under judgment stifles growth, it prevents us from admitting the error of our ways, learning from our mistakes, and from embracing the mercy that God offers us. We become selfish, closed minded, stuck in a quagmire of indecision and unable to move on. We experience a death of sort.

Historically, societies that have embraced judgment as the primary means of maintaining order have often been marked by division, violence, and stagnation. Religious persecution, oppressive legal systems, and warfare all find their roots in the human tendency to judge others harshly. When we prioritise judgment over connection, we foster environments where walls go up and Peace can no way flourish. The world is full of examples of communities torn apart by judgment, whether through racial discrimination, religious intolerance, or social inequalities.

The Better Tree:
A Life of Continuous Growth
and Peace

The Tree of Life, in contrast, represents the path of continuous growth and Peace. To choose the better tree is to choose a life where we are constantly being renewed by the Spirit of God, because better comes from God and draws us nearer to Him. Rather than focusing on who is right or wrong? We begin to focus on what is better for all? The focus becomes more on how we can grow, improve, and learn better how to become more aligned with God's will and each other. This path of seeking better encourages wisdom and grace, humility, and a commitment to reconciliation and lifelong learning.

In John 15:5, Jesus describes Himself as the true vine, saying, "I am the vine; you are the branches. If you remain in me and I in you, you will bear much fruit; apart from me, you can do nothing." Here, Jesus illustrates the importance of remaining connected to Him, the source of all life and Peace. Better comes from God. As we stay rooted in Him, we are nourished by His Spirit, and we grow into His likeness, bearing the fruit of Peace, love, and reconciliation in our lives.

Choosing the better tree, and seeking better means that we are constantly moving toward growth rather than staying stuck in the past or worrying about the future. When we choose growth, we acknowledge that none of us have arrived at perfection, and we give ourselves and others room to grow, learn, improve, and get better. This is the essence of grace, allowing for transformation rather than condemning based on past mistakes.

The Apostle Paul, in Philippians 3:13-14, speaks of this continuous growth when he writes, "But one thing I do: Forgetting what is behind and straining toward what is ahead, I press on toward the goal to win the prize for which God has called me heavenward in Christ Jesus." In this passage, Paul highlights the importance of focusing on what better lies ahead, on the process of becoming more like Christ, rather than being bound by past failures or judgments.

Grace and Unity:
Building a Peaceful Community

A key aspect of choosing the better tree is embracing grace, truth, and unity while consistently seeking better. Grace allows us to approach each other not with judgment but with compassion, understanding we are all on a journey of growth and all have something to share. Unity is the fruit of this grace, as it brings people together in the Spirit of Peace, despite their differences.

In Ephesians 4:2-3, Paul urges the Church to "Be completely humble and gentle; be patient, bearing with one another in love. Make every effort to keep the unity of the Spirit in the bond of Peace." Unity in the Church, and in any community, is not something that happens by accident. It requires intentional effort to stay humble, patient, and committed to Peace. It also requires us to abandon the need to judge or criticize others. To seek what's better for all, not what makes us better than others.

When communities live under the better tree, they become places of healing, reconciliation, restoration, and research. Everything is always getting better. Rather than creating divisions based on who is right or wrong, communities become spaces where people are encouraged to grow, to be vulnerable, and to see mistakes as opportunities to grab hold of better, and to seek understanding rather than hiding in shame.

This kind of community reflects the heart of Jesus, who welcomed sinners, forgave enemies, and sought to bring people together under the banner of God's Peace.

The metaphor of the better tree also extends to the way we deal with conflict. Instead of immediately judging or punishing those who do us wrong, we seek reconciliation, understanding, empathy, and grace.

Matthew 18:21-22 illustrates this when Peter asks Jesus, "Lord, how many times shall I forgive my brother or sister who sin against me? Up to seven times?" Jesus responds, "I tell you, not seven times, but seventy times seventy times." In other words, forgiveness is not a one-time event but a continual practice, just as personal growth and Peace are continual journeys.

The Role of the Holy Spirit in Cultivating Peace

The Holy Spirit is central to our ability to choose the better tree and live a life of continuous growth in Peace. In our own strength, we are often drawn back to judgment, criticism, and division. But the Spirit empowers us to live differently, to ask, "What is better?" And embrace grace, unity in endeavour, and ask what's better for all.

Galatians 5:22-23 reminds us that the fruit of the Spirit includes Peace, patience, kindness, and goodness. These fruits are cultivated in our lives as we remain grafted into Jesus and allow the Holy Spirit to work within and amongst us.

The Holy Spirit guides us into all truth (John 16:13), helping us discern what is better in each situation, rather than simply determining what is right or wrong. The Spirit gives us the humility to admit our own mistakes, the grace to forgive others, and the wisdom to seek new truths toward a better way forward for all, rather than retaliation or retribution.

In communities that are led by the Spirit, Peace flourishes. People are drawn together by a shared commitment to growth and grace, rather than divided by judgment or criticism. Better can bridge the gap between right from wrong with something new and improved for all.

Many can be one in endeavour, and what many believe many will do. Colossians 3:15 calls us to "let the Peace of Christ rule in your hearts, since as members of one body you were called to Peace. And be thankful." This passage emphasizes that Peace is not merely the void of war; it is the active presence of Christ in our hearts and communities, guiding us toward unity and love, as many can be one in the same like-minded direction.

Rejecting Judgment for a Life of Growth and Reconciliation

To live under the better tree is to reject judgment and embrace growth in new and better truths as we aim for reconnection amongst us. This means we choose to focus on how we can improve, how we can better love and serve others, and how we can live more fully in God's Peace. James 2:13 tells us that "mercy triumphs over judgment." When we choose mercy, when we offer grace and understanding instead of condemnation and shame, we are choosing the path of the better tree, the path that leads to continuous growth in excellence, constantly improving, and a Peace for all. (Psalm 37:37)

This approach to life, of seeking better rather than judging right from wrong, transforms our relationships within our communities and beyond, into our broader wider world. It allows us to build communities of Peace, where people feel safe to be vulnerable, to grow, and to learn from their mistakes without fear of judgment or shame poured upon them. It creates environments where connection is the goal, not retribution. Aligning ourselves with the heart of God means prioritising mercy over judgment and choosing unity and harmony over division. It means understanding none of us are beyond the need for grace, and none of us are beyond the reach of God's Peace. The better tree symbolises this life-giving path, one where each person is given the opportunity to grow in the image of Christ, rather than being condemned or shamed by their past.

Reconciliation is not only a personal act but a communal one. As we practice grace in our relationships, we help to cultivate cultures of peace and building better communities founded on Peace rather than violence or force. We become part of the solution to the world's divisions by living out the Peace of Christ. This commitment to growth over judgment fosters environments where conflicts are resolved through dialogue and understanding gained in empathy, rather than through force or exclusion. As Colossians 3:13 instructs, "Bear with each other and forgive one another, if any of you has a grievance against someone. Forgive as the Lord forgave you."

In this sense, choosing the better tree and seeking what is better for all is not just about avoiding conflict or choosing personal peace. It's about actively cultivating Peace in our communities by fostering reconciliation and unity in a better way forward for all. The fruits of this Peace ripple outwards, transforming people, families, neighbourhoods, churches, and even nations. This path of continuous growth creates opportunities for people to become their best selves, and for communities to experience God's heaven here on Earth.

The Holy Spirit empowers us to live in this Peace by continuously working within us to renew our hearts and minds. We must rely on the Holy Spirit to lead us into all truth and kindness, to guide us into joy in moments of struggle, and to fill us with the wisdom and patience needed to foster Peace rather than separation. When the Spirit leads, we become vessels of Peace, able to discern God's will and navigate the complexities of life in truth with grace and wisdom.

When we are grafted in to the Holy Spirit, our actions are no longer dictated by fear, pride, or the desire for control. Instead, we are led by the Spirit to respond in joy with love and humility, even in situations where our ego/self might urge us to judge or retaliate in anger. This reliance on the Holy Spirit brings about inner transformation, changing the way we approach conflict, and opening our hearts to God's will for unity and regeneration.

The fruit of the Spirit (Galatians 5:22-23) naturally flows from a life lived under the better tree. When we allow the Spirit to guide us, we are continually growing in Peace, patience, kindness, and love. The Spirit helps us to see others through the eyes of Christ, rather than from our own understanding, seeing their potential for growth, their inherent dignity, and their worth as human beings and children of God. This vision allows us to embrace Peace and reject judgment.

Summary:

As we conclude this chapter, we have looked into the metaphor of the better tree and how choosing growth over judgment leads us to a life of Peace and grace. We no longer need to hold on to being right, gladly passing it up for His better hope and expected end. (Jeremiah 29:11) Rejecting judgment is not about ignoring justice; rather, it is about embracing the path of progress, where people and communities are given the opportunity to grow and improve. The better tree symbolizes continuous growth, grace, and unity in endeavour, made possible through the Holy Spirit's work in our hearts and minds.

In Chapter 5: Living in Peace: Rejecting Force, Embracing Faith, we will explore how living in Peace requires us to reject the doctrine of "Peace by force" and instead embrace faith in God's provision. We will delve into how faith leads us to trust in God's ways over our own, allowing us to live in reconciliation and forgiveness, and to practice Peace in our daily lives. The next chapter will build on the themes of grace and growth, showing how faith empowers us to walk in Peace without relying on force or domination.

Group Study Questions

1. How does the metaphor of the better tree reflect the difference between living in judgment and living in grace?

2. What role does continuous growth play in our spiritual lives, and how does it align with the Peace that Jesus offers?

3. How can we see opportunity as 'for all' rather than for me alone?

4. How does the Holy Spirit empower us to live in Peace, and what steps can we take to rely more fully on the Spirit's guidance?

5. Joke: Why is it so hot in hell? There's no prayer conditioning.

Practical Applications:

Remaining in Peace:

Remaining in Peace requires continual dependence on God's presence and His promises. It's not just a passive state of being, but an active pursuit of aligning ourselves with God's will daily. In moments when anxiety or judgment threatens to overtake us, we are called to surrender our burdens to God and allow Him to fill us with His Peace. Isaiah 26:3 says, "God will keep in perfect Peace those whose minds are steadfast, because they trust in Him."

A practical way to remain in Peace is to begin each day with prayer, asking the Holy Spirit to guide your thoughts and actions. Consider making a habit of thanksgiving in prayer; by focusing on the blessings God has already provided, with this in mind you create a mindset of Peace and trust. Reflect on Isaiah 26:3 each morning as a way to centre your thoughts on God's steadfast Peace, particularly starting in the Amplified Bible Version. (AMP)

Living in Peace:

Living in Peace means being an instrument of God's Peace in your relationships and surroundings. It's not simply about avoiding conflict but about actively promoting Peace and reconciliation where there is discord. This requires humility, forgiveness, and a conscious decision to extend grace to others.

Living in Peace also means learning to speak Peace into situations of tension or misunderstanding. For example, instead of reacting defensively in an argument, choose to listen and empathise and respond with grace. You can practice living in Peace by pursuing regeneration with those from whom you have been estranged, following the example of Esau and Jacob, who embraced reconciliation despite their long-standing conflict.

Walking with His Peace:

Walking with His Peace requires a steady trust in God's promises, even when circumstances around us seem chaotic. It is a continual practice of faith, believing that God's Peace is not based on outward conditions but on the unshakable truth of His love and sovereignty. Psalm 23:4 reminds us, "Even though walking through the darkest valley, I will fear no evil, for you are with me and promise to comfort me."

In practical terms, this means seeking to bring Peace into every environment you enter. Whether at work, in your family, your school or in your community, walk with the mindset that you are an ambassador of Christ's Peace. When you encounter conflict or stress, take a moment to pause and seek God's guidance before responding. A quick, simple little prayer can help, "Lord, Peace be upon those who drive me crazy." Reflect on Psalm 23 as a reminder that no matter the situation, God's Peace is with you, guiding and protecting you.

Recommended Bible Reading:
Genesis 33:1-11 −The Reconciliation of Esau and Jacob

In this powerful story, Jacob, who had deceived his brother Esau years earlier, returns home fearing his brother's anger. However, instead of seeking revenge, Esau embraces Jacob with love and forgiveness. The two brothers, once estranged, are reconciled through humility and grace. This story beautifully illustrates how Peace and healing can emerge from what seems like an irreparably broken relationship, showing that reconciliation is always possible when we are willing to let go of the wrongs of the past.

This story challenges us to trust in God's ability to transform hearts and reminds us that even deep family feuds can be healed. It emphasizes the role of forgiveness and reconciliation in restoring Peace, both within families and within communities.

Chapter 5

Living in Peace Rejecting Force Embracing Faith

The False Doctrine of "Peace by Force"

For much of human history, Peace has often been equated with the ability to overpower one's enemies. This philosophy of "Peace by superior firepower," as explored in previous chapters, is built on the idea true Peace is only achievable when one possesses the power to coerce others into submission. Governments, nations, and individuals alike have long believed that violence, intimidation, and force are necessary tools for maintaining Peace and order. But this concept is fundamentally at odds with the teachings of Jesus Christ, who offers a radically different vision for achieving and sustaining Peace.

In this chapter, we will explore the fallacy of Peace by force and how faith, not coercion, is central to living in the Peace left to us in accepting Jesus' offer of reconciliation with God and mankind. Living in Peace requires a deep reliance on God's guidance and the conviction that His ways, though often at odds with our human instincts, are always better than any strategy based on force, power, strife, or domination. Rejecting force does not mean ignoring injustice or allowing harm to flourish, but it calls for us to trust in God's ultimate justice and embrace His method of reconnection, new truth, new life, and renewing love.

Trusting God to Bring True Peace Through Faith

Faith, at its core, is about trusting in the unseen. Faith is what we do with what we believe to be true. It's believing in God's promises even when our surroundings suggest otherwise. Jesus taught Peace doesn't come from the ability to control others or eliminate conflict through sheer force, but from a heart trusting God's plan over humanly programs. It is a new truth that sets us free from our past. In John 8:31-32, Jesus says to those who believe, if you continue in my word, then you are my disciples indeed, and you shall know the truth, and the truth shall set you free. In John 20:29, Jesus says, "Thomas, because you have seen, you have believed, blessed are they that have not seen, and yet still believe."

In contrast to the world's approach to Peace, which is often grounded in fear, violence, and control, the Peace of Jesus is grounded in faith, a trust in God's sovereignty and a commitment to His kingdom's principles. John 14:27 records Jesus' comforting words: "Peace I leave with you; my Peace I give to you. I do not give to you as the world gives. Don't let your hearts be troubled and do not be afraid." Jesus offers a Peace that is not subject to the tumult of the world, but one that is deeply anchored in God's eternal will.

To live in this gift of Peace, we must learn to reject our human tendencies toward control and coercion and instead embrace the Peace that comes through faith. Matthew 5:9

declares, "Blessed are the Peacemakers, for they will be called children of God." This statement reveals the deeper truth that Peacemaking is an act of faith, a belief God's way of Peace through love and reconnecting kindness, will ultimately prevail over the ways of war and domination.

Consider the Israelites during their exodus from Egypt. As they stood at the edge of the Red Sea, pursued by Pharaoh's army, many of them panicked, crying out in fear. But Moses reminded them to trust in God's deliverance, saying, "The LORD will fight for you; you need only to be still" (Exodus 14:14). This moment encapsulates the essence of faith-based Peace: when everything around us calls for action, retaliation, or fear, God often calls us to be still and trust in Him.

Rejecting Force:
The Example of Jesus

Throughout His ministry, Jesus consistently rejected the use of force to accomplish His mission. Whether dealing with religious authorities, Roman rulers, or His own disciples, Jesus chose the path of non-violence and faith in God's plan. One of the clearest examples of this is found in Matthew 26:52, when Jesus is arrested in the Garden of Gethsemane. As one of His disciples draws a sword to defend Him, Jesus rebukes the action, saying, "Put your sword back in its place, for all who draw the sword will die by the sword."

In this intensely critical moment, Jesus demonstrates His commitment to rejecting force. He could have called on legions of angels to defend Him, but instead, He willingly submitted to His Father's plan, trusting that God's will would be accomplished through His sacrifice, not through violence. His refusal to resort to force, even when His life was at stake, is a powerful reminder faith in God's purpose is the bedrock of true Peace.

Likewise, Jesus taught His followers to turn the other cheek, love their enemies, and pray for those who persecuted them (Matthew 5:39-44). These teachings were revolutionary at the time, and they remain counter-cultural today. Jesus wasn't advocating for passivity in the face of injustice, but rather for proactive faith that trusts in God's ability to bring about justice and Peace in ways that transcend human methods of control and violence.

Living in Reconciliation and Forgiveness

One of the key ways that Jesus demonstrated His Peace was through His commitment to reconciliation, grace, and forgiveness. The world often seeks Peace by forcing adversaries into submission, but Jesus sought Peace by reconciling enemies and extending forgiveness. In Luke 23:34, even as He hung on the cross, Jesus prayed, "Father, forgive them, for they do not know what they are doing." This profound act of forgiveness, in the midst of excruciating pain and injustice, reveals the depth of Jesus' commitment to Peace through reconciliation.

Living in Peace, therefore, requires us to practice grace and forgiveness in our daily lives. Forgiveness is not easy. It requires humility, grace, and a willingness to let go of our "natural" desire for revenge or control. Jesus teaches forgiveness as the new "natural" intrinsic and essential to Peace.

In Matthew 18:21-22, when Peter asks how many times, Lord, must I forgive someone who sins against me, Jesus responds, "I tell you, not seven times, but seventy times seven times." This statement underscores the limitless nature of forgiveness in the kingdom of God.

Forgiveness is a powerful act of faith because it requires us to trust in God's justice and to release our need for personal retribution. We have to willingly accept the consequences of someone else's mistake. When we forgive, we open the door for God's Peace to enter into our heart and flow out into our relationships. Colossians 3:13 reminds us, "Bear with each other and forgive one another, if any of you has a grievance against someone, forgive as the Lord has forgiven you." In forgiving others, we mirror the Peace Jesus offers, allowing love and mateship to replace control, conflict, and division.

Faith-Based Peace in Daily Life

Living in Peace by faith means rejecting the world's narrative that power and force are necessary for survival. Instead, it means trusting God's way of Peace, through love, humility, forgiving kindness and grace, is not only possible but transformative. Peace is a prerequisite to human survival. This requires a daily commitment to surrender our fears and rely on God's provision.

One way we can practice this in our daily lives is by choosing to respond to conflict with grace rather than force. Whether in personal relationships, professional settings, or larger social contexts, we are often tempted to use coercion, manipulation, or bullying aggression to achieve our desired outcomes. But faith-based Peace calls us to reject these methods and instead seek wisdom, understanding, dialogue, reconciliation, and unity of Spirit.

In our modern world, it can feel as though Peace is impossible to maintain without some degree of control or domination. But when we trust God, we are freed from the burden of needing to be right and to control everything. Obviously, there is law and order, however in the spirit of, rather than to the letter of.

Philippians 4:6-7 tells us, "Do not be anxious about anything, but in every situation, by prayer and petition, with thanksgiving, present your requests to God. And the Peace of God, which transcends all understanding, will guard your hearts and your minds in Christ Jesus." This Peace, which goes beyond human understanding, is the reward for those who live in faith.

Summary:

As we close this chapter, we have explored how living in Peace requires us to reject force and instead embrace faith in God's plan and better way. Through reconciliation, forgiveness, and trust, we can live out the Peace that Jesus modelled. This Peace is not passive but is an active, faith-filled response to the conflicts and challenges we face in our everyday lives. It is a Peace firmly grounded in the belief God's ways are of Peace toward us, and are of a higher order than our own. Jesus is the ultimate source of Peace, justice, and salvation. Jesus is the good news of the grace of God.

In Chapter 6: The Golden Rule For All: A Framework for Peace, we will explore how the Golden Rule, to treat others equally as we would want to be fairly treated, serves as a practical framework for living in Peace. This teaching of Jesus offers a powerful blueprint for building relationships and communities that are grounded in mutual respect, compassion, and Peace.

Practical Applications:
Remaining in Peace:

To remain in Peace, especially in a world filled with anxiety and unrest, it's crucial to focus on God's faithfulness rather than on our own circumstances. This means trusting God is in control, even when life feels hectic or chaotic. Rejoice! Nehemiah 8:10, suggests the joy of the Lord is our strength and Isaiah 30:15 reminds us, "In repentance and rest is your salvation, in quietness and trust is your strength." The more we cultivate a life of prayer and reflection, the more we can remain in God's Peace, knowing that He fights our battles, carries our burdens, and releases new truths for our salvation.

A practical way to stay grounded in Peace is to make meditations on scripture a daily practice. Start each morning by reading and reflecting on verses that remind you of God's promises. As you do this, ask the Holy Spirit to help you internalise these truths, so that you can remain in Peace even when trials come. Let Philippians 4:6-7 guide your prayers, and remember that God's Peace will guard your heart when you surrender your anxieties to Him.

Living in Peace:

Living in Peace requires an active commitment to promoting Peace and harmony in your relationships and interactions with other people and groups. It involves rejecting aggression, manipulation, control, or force as a means of achieving our outcomes, and instead, choosing humility and staying in the unity of endeavour. In your daily life, this could look like offering a calm and compassionate response when faced with criticism or unfair treatment, trusting that God will vindicate you in due time. Proverbs 15:1, "A gentle answer turns away wrath, but a harsh word stirs up anger."

Another practical way to live in Peace is by fostering patience and understanding in your relationships. We can all become better listeners and empathise more. We can practice listening to hear rather than to respond. When conflicts arise, resist the urge to control the situation by force or coercion. Instead, pause, take a breath, hold it, and breathe, pray, and seek the Holy Spirit's guidance on how to respond with grace. Ask yourself, "How can I honour God by seeking unity of Spirit instead of retaliation?"

Walking with His Peace:

Walking with Christ's Peace is a lifelong journey of faith. It means learning to trust God's timing and His methods, even when they don't align with our own. As we walk with His Peace, we become less reactive to the world around us and more grounded in His unchanging truth. Psalm 37:7 advises us to "Be still before the Lord and wait patiently for him; do not fret when people succeed in their ways, when they carry out their wicked schemes." Walking with His Peace means knowing God is sovereign and His justice will prevail.

In practical terms, walking with His Peace may involve practicing restraint in moments of tension. Instead of rushing to defend yourself or to assert control, take a step back and seek God's wisdom. Walking in Peace is about learning to trust God's process of restoration, knowing true Peace cannot be achieved through human effort alone, but through faith in God's perfect plan for Peace, His Son Jesus Christ.

Group Study Questions

1. Joke: Jesus walks into a motel, puts a handful of nails onto the desk and says, "Can ya put me up for the night?"
2. How does the world's concept of Peace differ from the Peace that Jesus offers through faith?
3. What role does faith play in rejecting force and embracing reconciliation and forgiveness?
4. In what ways can we practice faith-based Peace in our daily lives, particularly in moments of conflict or tension?
5. How can we look at opportunity through the eyes of care rather than advantage?

Recommended Bible Reading:
Exodus 14:1-31 – Moses and the Red Sea

This passage shows the importance of trusting in God during moments of fear and uncertainty. When the Israelites faced an impossible situation, trapped between the Red Sea and Pharaoh's army, God delivered them not through force, but through faith and obedience. Moses' command to "be still" teaches us that Peace comes when we rely on God's intervention, rather than our own strength.

Luke 5:17-26 –Jesus Forgives and Heals a Paralysed Man

In this story, we see Jesus not only healing a man's physical affliction but also addressing the deeper need for spiritual healing through forgiveness. The act of forgiving the man's sin before healing his body highlights how Peace begins in the soul, reconciling spirit with God. It is a reminder that Peace requires spiritual healing, and forgiveness is the first step toward restoration and wholeness.

John 11: 38-44 –Loose the grave clothes

Jesus stood before the tomb and commanded the stone to be removed. Martha doubted because decay had set in. Jesus prayed and cried out; Lazarus come forth. At His word, life returned and Lazarus arose still bound. In the same way, the church, though weakened, must hear His call, rise in His power, and be loosed from the grave clothes of dead tradition. Life is in Christ alone.

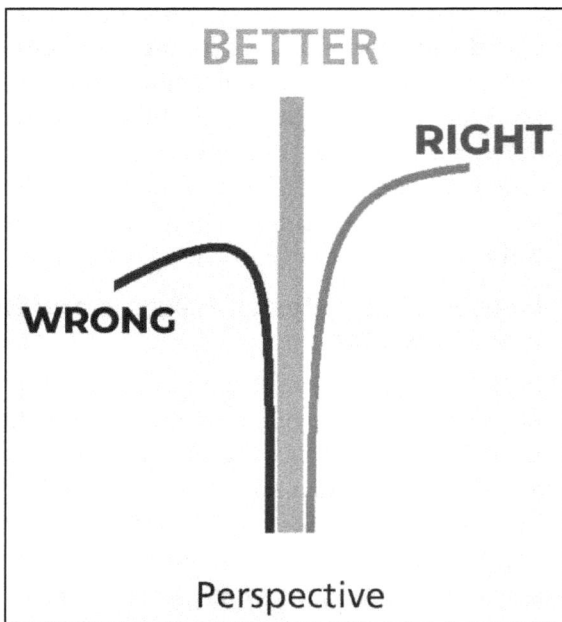

BETTER

RIGHT

WRONG

Perspective

Here is right. There is wrong. However
better never ends in improving upon all
things. Better makes all things new again.

Chapter 6

The Golden Rule for All:
A Framework for Peace

The Foundation of
Faith-Based Peace

In Chapter 5, we explored the radical shift Jesus calls us to embrace by rejecting force and embracing faith. We saw how Peace is not achieved through domination or control but through reliance on God's way, grounded in trust and reconciliation. This understanding of Peace sets the stage for a deeper examination of how we are called to live out this Peace daily through the lens of the Golden Rule.

The Golden Rule, as taught by Jesus, offers a practical framework for living in Peace. It is a simple yet profoundly transformative principle: "Do unto others equally as you would have them do unto you" (Matthew 7:12). This command is not just a guideline for personal morality, but a blueprint for building relationships and communities that reflect the heart of God's kingdom. In this chapter, we will explore how the Golden Rule for all, serves as the foundation for Peace within ourselves, and our relationships, the broader community and across the world, simply drawing upon the teachings and example of Jesus.

The Golden Rule calls us to act with empathy, compassion, and respect, fundamentally rejecting the self-centredness that leads to conflict and division, that being, our own self-righteousness through the lens of our own understanding. Jesus warns us about the abomination causing desolation sitting in high places. (Matthew 24:15) By treating others with the same dignity we desire for ourselves, we reflect the gospel of Peace, fostering harmony in our relationships and in our communities. This rule goes beyond merely preventing harm, it actively promotes healing, unity, and love. In this chapter, we will unpack the implications of the Golden Rule as a framework for Peace and explore how daily we can proactively live in Peace together, to deliver the golden rule to all.

The Universal Power of the Golden Rule

The Golden Rule is one of the most universally recognized and generally accepted ethical principles across cultures and religions. Its simplicity and depth have made it a cornerstone of moral teaching throughout history, yet its power is fully realized only when understood through the lens of Jesus' kingdom of Peace. In His ministry, Jesus not only reiterated the Golden Rule for all but elevated it as the heart of His teachings on love, charity, and forgiveness.

When Jesus taught the Golden Rule in Matthew 7:12, He did so within the context of the Sermon on the Mount, a series of teachings that entirely redefined the meaning of righteousness and honest living. Jesus is not merely asking people to follow a moral code. He is inviting people to participate in the kingdom of God. Where relationships are not defined by power dynamics, but by love, kindness, and mutual respect.

The Golden Rule is a direct reflection of God's nature. It encapsulates His desire for His people to live in harmony, to seek the well-being of others, and to embody His love in tangible ways. Philippians 2:3-4 underscores this, calling us to "Do nothing out of selfish ambition or vain conceit. Rather, in humility, value others above yourselves, not looking to your own interests but each of you to the interests of others." The Golden Rule is about seeing others through the eyes of Christ and responding with the same grace and mercy that we have received from Him.

Jesus embodied the Golden Rule for all, throughout His life consistently prioritizing the needs of others, and demonstrating compassion toward those who were marginalized or oppressed. His healing of the sick, His forgiveness of sinners, and His willingness to serve even those who opposed Him, all reflect the principle of treating others as we ourselves would want to be fairly treated. The Golden Rule for all is therefore more than a command, it is the ethic of the kingdom of God, the framework through which we participate in His work of reconciliation, Peace, and goodwill to all.

How the Golden Rule Transforms Conflict

At its core, the Golden Rule for all, transforms the way we approach conflict. In a world that often promotes retaliation, competition, and self-interest, the Golden Rule for all offers a different path, one of empathy, understanding and opportunity paved with generosity, kindness, and unity in the endeavour of fairness. Instead of seeking to dominate or win over others in moments of tension, the Golden Rule calls us to ask: How would I want to be treated in this situation? This simple question invites a profound shift in our behaviour, moving us from a place of defensiveness to one of understanding through empathy.

Matthew 18:15-17 offers a practical application of the Golden Rule in the context of conflict resolution within the church. Jesus teaches us if someone sins against us, we should go to them privately and seek reconciliation. This approach reflects the Golden Rule because it prioritises restoration over punishment. Rather than publicly shaming or retaliating, seeking retribution against the person who has wronged us, we are called to engage them with the goal of restoring relationship. This reflects how we would want to be treated if we were the one at fault.

The Golden Rule also transforms interpersonal conflicts by encouraging us to listen, to empathize, and to seek peaceful resolutions. Encouraging acts of kindness. James 1:19 reminds us, "Everyone should be quick to listen, slow to speak, and slower to become angry." Applying the Golden Rule for all in moments of conflict means being slow to anger, quick to listen, and willing to understand the other person's perspective. By doing so, we create space for dialogue and healing rather than perpetuating the cycle of hostility.

In larger societal conflicts, the Golden Rule offers a framework for addressing injustice and promoting Peaceful change. It challenges us to consider the needs of the oppressed and marginalized, asking how we would want to be treated if we were in their situation. Isaiah 1:17 suggests to live honest lives, seek justice, and defend the oppressed." This call to justice is inherently tied to the Golden Rule, as it requires us to advocate for those whose voices are unheard and whose dignity is disqualified or denied.

Bringing the Golden Rule to Life in Our Communities

The Golden Rule is not just an abstract principle but a practical guide for building Peaceful communities. When lived out, it has the power to transform not only individual relationships but entire communities, fostering a culture of humility, respect, thankfulness for salvation, mutual benefit, and Peace. The golden rule cultivates a culture of Peace. In a community where the Golden Rule is embraced, there is no room for violence, exploitation, or prejudice, because each person is seen as a mate, a reflection of God's image, child of the living God, citizen of Peace, deserving of dignity, love, respect, and kindness simply for being a DNA proven individual human being.

In practice, living out the Golden Rule for all in our communities means making a conscious effort to treat every person we encounter with the same level of respect and kindness that we would desire for ourselves. It means advocating for the powerless, voiceless, and vulnerable, supporting those in need, and speaking out against injustice. Proverbs 31:8-9 commands us to "Speak up for those who cannot speak for themselves, for the rights of all who are destitute. Voice up and judge fairly; defend the rights of the poor and needy."

In a community shaped by the Golden Rule, diversity is celebrated rather than feared, and differences are seen as opportunities for learning and growth, rather than as threats. The early church provides an example of such a community, where people from different backgrounds and social classes came together to share their resources and care for one another's needs (Acts 2:44-47). This was not just an expression of charity, it was performing the Golden Rule, where each person's well-being was treated as equally important as one's own.

In our modern context, this might look like creating spaces where dialogue and understanding are prioritised over judgment. It means being willing to extend grace to those who think or act differently from us, and to pursue reconciliation when conflicts arise. Living out the Golden

Rule requires us to cultivate an attitude of service and to seek ways to uplift and support others in tangible ways. Hebrews 5:8-9, Though he was a Son, yet learned he obedience by the things which he suffered; And being made perfect, he became the author of eternal salvation unto all them that obey him;

After doing no wrong, and still being punished and harmed to teach him a lesson, Jesus goes on to perfect new truths being fundamental to salvation rather than the use of harm to correct. His Peace mentors us in better ways not punish us or bring harm to teach us lessons. The Golden Rule cultivates a better civility than teaching someone a lesson by causing them harm.

Practical Applications:

Remaining in Peace:

Remaining in Peace requires daily mindfulness of how we treat others, recognizing that Peace begins within us and extends outward. In our moments of tension or irritation, the Golden Rule calls us to pause and ask ourselves: How would I want to be treated in this situation? Reflecting on this can help calm our hearts and guide us to respond with love and grace, rather than frustration and in anger or harshness. Romans 12:18 encourages us, "If it is possible, as far as it depends on you, live in Peace with everyone."

A practical way to remain in Peace is to incorporate this principle into your daily routine. At the start of each day, pray for the Holy Spirit to guide your interactions, asking specifically for the wisdom to apply the Golden Rule in difficult situations. Throughout your day, whenever you face a challenge, conflict, or struggle, take a moment to reflect on how you would want to be treated and use that as a guide for your response. Let Philippians 4:7 remind you the Peace of God, which transcends all understanding, will guard your heart and mind in Christ Jesus.

Living in Peace:

Living in Peace requires us to actively pursue reconciliation and to show kindness and patience to others, particularly in times of conflict. This means not just avoiding harm, but actively seeking the well-being of those around us. Proverbs 15:1 tells us, "A gentle answer turns away wrath, but a harsh word stirs up anger." Harshness is a weakness, not a strength. Kindness is a strength and not a weakness as some may consider. Living in Peace according to the Golden Rule for all often means being the first to extend a gentle word, even when you feel wronged.

To live this out, make it a goal to initiate Peace in your relationships. If you find yourself in a disagreement, practice active listening, showing the other person their thoughts and feelings matter, just as you would want yours to be equally respected. By doing so, you embody the Peace of Christ, bringing calm to situations that might otherwise escalate into strife or violent conflict rather than a resolve. The Golden Rule for all, in practice, means choosing to de-escalate rather than escalate, it means not retaliating but seeking common ground, reconnection, and single endeavour.

Walking with His Peace:

Walking with His Peace means embodying the Golden Rule not just in isolated situations, but as a way of life. It involves a conscientious and enthusiastic conscious commitment to be a Peacemaker wherever you go, whether at home, school, at work, or in your community. Walking in Peace is about carrying Christ's love with you in every interaction, making Peace not only a response but a guiding principle in all that you do.

Colossians 3:15 encourages us to "let the Peace of Christ rule in your hearts." This implies that Peace is not passive but something we must intentionally allow to govern our thoughts and actions. As you go about your day, make it a practice to ask: How can I bring Peace into this situation? Whether it's by offering a word of encouragement, stepping in to mediate a conflict, or simply showing kindness to a stranger, walking in Peace can transform your daily encounters and reflect the heart of Christ.

Let the Golden Rule serve as your guide. Each time you're unsure how to proceed, pause and listen to you breathe, come back to the moment, and ask how you would want to be treated. This simple shift in perspective can lead to profound changes in how you relate to others and how you experience the Peace of Christ in your own life.

Up Next:

Reviewing this chapter, we have explored how the Golden Rule serves as a powerful framework for living in Peace, peaceably together. By treating others as we would want to be treated, we align ourselves with the heart of Jesus' kingdom, where relationships are built on love, respect, and compassion. The Golden Rule is not merely a moral guideline but a call to participate in God's work of Peace, reconciliation, healing, and grace in the world.

In Chapter 7: Peace for a Broken World, we will turn our attention to how this framework of Peace can be applied to some of the most pressing issues of our time, specifically the structural violence that impacts vulnerable populations. We will explore how Jesus' teachings on Peace offer hope and healing for those who have been oppressed and marginalized, and how we are called to be agents of His Peace in a broken world.

Group Study Questions

1. How does the Golden Rule for all serve as a practical framework for living in Peace in our daily relationships and communities?
2. In what ways can the Golden Rule transform conflicts, both personal and societal?
3. How can we actively bring the Golden Rule to life in our communities, particularly in areas of injustice and inequality?
4. How can the Golden Rule for all prevent people from taking advantage of others simply because they can?

Recommended Bible Reading:

Luke 10:25-37 –The Good Samaritan

This parable powerfully illustrates the Golden Rule in action. The Samaritan, who was adversely considered by the Jews of the day, shows compassion and care for a wounded man when others pass by. Despite their cultural differences, the Samaritan treats the injured man with the same kindness and care that he would want for himself. Jesus uses this story to demonstrate that our neighbours are not just those who are close to us, but anyone in need of love and compassion, regardless of cultural differences. This story is a profound example of how applying the Golden Rule for all transcends societal boundaries and can bring healing, justice, and Peace.

1 Samuel 25:14-35 –Abigail Intervenes to Prevent David's Wrath

Abigail's wisdom and quick action prevented bloodshed when her husband Nabal insulted David. Instead of escalating the conflict, Abigail humbly approached David with gifts and pleaded for peace. Her actions exemplify how applying the Golden Rule of treating others with dignity, humility, and respect, can defuse tension and bring about reconciliation and restoration. Abigail's choice to put herself in David's shoes and anticipate how he would want to be treated, ultimately preserved peace, and prevented violence. This story shows the how the power of empathetic intervention in tense situations can ease hostility and prevent conflict.

Luke 9:37-44 –Healing hearts and minds

Jesus calls us to deny ourselves, lay down our ego, and take up His cross daily. In surrender, we receive His Peace, the Spirit of Truth and find true healing. Not just of our body, or church, but healing our hearts and mind as well. Losing ourselves in Him, we gain life. His kingdom within us brings heaven to Earth and reveals His power and glory for all to see.

Chapter 7

Peace for a Broken World

The Brokenness of Our World

In the previous chapter, we examined the Golden Rule as a framework for living in Peace, calling us to treat others with the same compassion and respect we desire for ourselves. But in a world deeply fractured by systemic injustice and structural violence, living out this command often requires more than individual acts of kindness. It requires confronting and healing the systems of oppression that dehumanize and marginalize the vulnerable, especially women and children.

Throughout history, women and children have been among the most vulnerable populations, often bearing the brunt of much violence, exploitation, prejudice, and discrimination. From human trafficking, forced labour and domestic abuse to institutionalised gender inequality, the forces of oppression have created deep wounds that demand a healing in response. The teachings of Jesus, instead, offer a radical alternative to these structures. Jesus' message of Peace is not passive, it's active, it is a revolutionary call to confront and heal the injustices that have been perpetuated by the world's broken systems. Jesus urges truth speaking to power to bring about the true justice of never again.

In this chapter, we will explore how Jesus' teachings, particularly those concerning equality, compassion, dignity, respect, and justice, provide a pathway to healing the structural violence particularly afflicting women and children. We will also examine the role of the Church and individual believers in promoting Peace and restoring dignity to those who have been marginalized and hurt.

Addressing the Structural Nature of Violence

Violence against women and children is not just a result of individual acts of cruelty. It is often founded in societal structures that normalize or perpetuate oppression. These structures can be cultural, legal, economic, or religious, and they create environments where violence is tolerated or even encouraged, as lessons to be learnt. Patriarchy, colonisation, and imperialism, for example, has historically placed women in subordinate roles, limiting their rights and subjecting them to control and violence. Similarly, children in many parts of the world are treated as property or labourers, rather than as individuals with inherent dignity and worth.

Jesus' teachings directly challenge these power dynamics and call for a new way of living that prioritises the value of every human being, regardless of their gender, age, status, or back story. In a society where women were often marginalized and children seen as insignificant or unimportant, Jesus consistently demonstrated a radical inclusivity and a willingness to uplift the voices and lives of the oppressed.

Consider Jesus' interactions with women in the Gospels. In a culture that had often viewed women as inferior, Jesus treated them with dignity, spoke to them in public (a radical act at the time), and involved them in His ministry. John 4:1-42 tells the story of Jesus' conversation with the Samaritan woman at the well. Not only did He speak to her, a Samaritan, and a woman with a troubled past, but He offered her the living water of eternal life and revealed His identity as the Messiah to her. Through this interaction, Jesus shattered the cultural and societal norms of His day and demonstrated that no one is beyond His love.

In the same way, Jesus elevated the status of children, who were often overlooked or dismissed. In Matthew 19:13-14, we see how Jesus welcomed children when His disciples tried to turn them away. "Let the little children come to me, and hinder them not, for the kingdom of heaven belongs to such as these." Here, Jesus not only embraces the children but declares that the kingdom of God belongs to those who come to Him with the innocence and openness of a child. In doing so, He affirms the dignity and worth of children, challenging the cultural assumptions of His time.

The Role of Jesus' Peace in Healing Societal Wounds

The Peace that Jesus offers is not merely the absence of conflict but the presence of justice. It is a Peace that encompasses wholeness, reconciliation, and restoration. His Peace seeks to heal the deep wounds caused by violence and oppression with a grace and love Jesus has for us. For women and children who have been subjected to systemic injustice, the Peace of Jesus offers hope for healing and renewal.

One of the most profound examples of Jesus' Peace confronting societal oppression is His response to the woman caught in adultery in John 8:1-11. In this story, the religious leaders bring a woman to Jesus, accusing her of adultery and demanding she be stoned according to the law of Moses, but not the bloke. Their intent is not only to punish her, but to trap Jesus. Instead of condemning her, Jesus responds with compassion and wisdom, saying, "Let any one of you who is without sin be the first to throw a stone at her." One by one, her accusers leave, and Jesus, the only one without sin, tells her, "Neither do I condemn you. Go now and live your life for good."

This encounter reveals the heart of Jesus' mission, to bring mercy where there is condemnation, to offer restoration where there is shame, and to protect the vulnerable from the violence of unjust systems. Jesus not only forgives the woman but restores her dignity, offering her a path to a new life free from both her past and the violence of her oppressors. This story serves as a powerful reminder that Jesus' Peace is not complacent, it is active in confronting injustice and bringing healing to those who have been hurt by the world's systems.

In our modern context, this means His Church must stand against the structural violence harming women and children, advocating for equality, fairness, justice, protection, respect, and restoration, rather than being excluded from ministry. Whether through addressing issues like domestic abuse, labour exploitation, slave trafficking, or gender-based discrimination, Church is called to be a voice for the voiceless and a force for Peace in a broken world.

Rejecting Harm as a Tool for Teaching Lessons

Society often justifies violence against women and children by framing it as a necessary tool for discipline or control. In many cultures, physical punishment is seen as an acceptable way to "teach lessons" or enforce obedience. However, this unhelpful mindset runs contrary to the teachings of Jesus, Lord of all, who consistently rejected violence as a means to achieving an end.

Proverbs 22:6 says, "Train up a child in the way he should go, and when he is old, he will not depart from it." This passage is often interpreted as an endorsement of strict discipline, but when viewed through the lens of Jesus' Peace, it becomes clear that training a child in the ways of the Lord should involve nurturing, teaching, guiding, and mentoring, rather than harming, bullying, or coercion. Jesus' approach to teaching was always founded in love, grace, and compassion, not force or intimidation.

Similarly, violence against women is often justified under the guise of maintaining order or enforcing authority within families or societies. However, the New Testament calls for an entirely different vision of relationship, one based on mutual respect, care, and sacrificial love. Ephesians 5:25 commands, husbands love your wives, just as Christ loves His church and gave himself up for her. This passage frames the relationship between men and women not as one of male dominance, but as one of self-giving love, where violence has no place.

Restoring Dignity and Protection Through Peace

The ultimate goal of Jesus' Peace is to restore dignity to those who have been dehumanized by violence and to create communities of protection where the vulnerable are cared for, not exploited. The Church, as the body of Christ, has a responsibility to advocate for Peace, for the rights and safety of women and children, providing both spiritual and practical support for those effecting, and those affected, by structural violence or cultural prejudice.

This might involve working in small groups in local churches to instigate a general renewal in behaviour and societal change toward doing Peace, with renewed insights and vigour into Peace and goodwill for all, and leading the way of reform in the proliferation of His Peace. Possibly working with local organizations to support survivors of abuse and crime, providing education and resources for women and children in underserved areas, or advocating for the legal reforms that will protect the rights of vulnerable people better. In doing these things, His Church becomes a visible manifestation of the gospel of God's Peace, offering hope and healing to those who have been wounded by the world's broken systems.

As we strive to live out Jesus' Peace, we need to remember that our actions are part of a larger story of redemption and restoration. We are called to be Peacemakers, creating environments where women, children and all vulnerable people can thrive, free from the violence that has plagued them for so long.

Summary:

In this chapter, we have explored how the Peace of Jesus confronts the structural violence that has harmed women, children, the outcasts and ostracized for generations. Through His teachings and actions, Jesus calls us to be agents of Peace, working to heal the deep wounds of bias and oppression and restore the dignity of those who have been dehumanized.

In Chapter 8, we will shift our focus to the broader social belief that violence and war are necessary for achieving Peace. We will explore how history has consistently shown the failure of this approach and examine how Jesus' message calls us to reject the false promises of war and instead embrace His vision of Peace through reconciliation, justice, and love. The next chapter challenges the notion that Peace can be achieved through force and invites us to trust in the Peace of Christ as the ultimate solution for a war-torn world.

Practical Applications:

Remaining in Peace:

Remaining in Peace requires constant awareness of the ways in which society dehumanizes the vulnerable, especially women and children. Take time daily to reflect on your role as a citizen of Peace. Consider how you can actively challenge the systemic injustices that perpetuate violence. James 1:27 reminds us, "Religion that God our Father accepts as pure and faultless is this: to look after orphans and widows in their distress." To remain in Peace, pray regularly for the wisdom and courage to stand against injustice and be an advocate for the marginalized.

Living in Peace:

Living in Peace means actively seeking a justice, of never again, which comes with the salvation of a better truth, as well as being a voice for the voiceless. Consider how you can be involved in local or global efforts to protect women and children from violence and exploitation. This could involve volunteering with organizations and groups supportive of survivors of abuse, that are advocating for legal reforms, or simply educating yourself and others about the issues that affect vulnerable people and populations particularly through your small group efforts. Living in Peace requires us to take action to address the fundamental causes of violence and creating spaces of safety, healing, and wellbeing.

Walking with His Peace:

Walking with His Peace means allowing Christ's heart for the oppressed to shape your daily actions and decisions. This includes advocating for fair treatment, providing support and encouragement to those in need, and seeking ways to be a light in the darkness of systemic violence. As you walk with His Peace, reflect on how you can offer compassion, empathy, and practical support to those who have been wounded by the world's broken systems. Ask yourself, what can I do today to bring the Peace of Jesus Christ to those among us who need it most?

Group Study Questions

1. How does Jesus' Peace challenge the structural violence that has historically harmed women, children, and vulnerable populations?
2. In what ways can the Church actively participate in bringing healing and protection to those affected by systemic violence?
3. How can Jesus' interactions with women and children in the Gospels serve as a model for how we treat the vulnerable in our communities today?
4. What are some practical steps we can take to advocate for justice and Peace in the face of societal systems that perpetuate violence?
5. Joke: What happened to the computer file that didn't believe in Jesus? It wasn't saved.

Recommended Bible Reading:
Genesis 16:1-16 –Hagar and the Angel of the Lord

Hagar, a woman marginalized and oppressed by her circumstances, encounters God in the wilderness.

When she flees from the mistreatment of her mistress, Sarah, God sends an angel to comfort and guide her. This story illustrates how God sees and cares for those who are mistreated and vulnerable, offering hope and protection when the world fails to provide it. Hagar's encounter with the divine reveals that no one is outside of God's love and care, especially the oppressed.

Mark 5:21-43 –The Healing of Jairus' Daughter and the Woman with the Issue of Blood

This powerful passage tells of two intertwined stories. Jesus heals a young girl, the daughter of Jairus, and simultaneously restores a woman who had been suffering for twelve years. Both women, one a child and the other an outcast, represent society's most vulnerable. Yet Jesus shows compassion and heals both, restoring their dignity and demonstrating that His Peace brings life, truth, and healing to those marginalized by societal structures.

Exodus 7-14 –The Exodus and the Plagues of Egypt

This story highlights how Pharaoh's reliance on force and oppression ultimately led to his downfall and the liberation of the Israelites. It emphasizes that power and violence cannot bring lasting Peace.

Luke 9: 23- 27 –The call to lay down our ego self

Jesus calls us to deny the ego self, take up His cross daily, and follow Him. True life is found in surrender to Him and service to others. What good is it to gain the world yet lose ourselves and loved ones to a self-centred ego?

Micah 4:3,

"And he shall judge among many people, and rebuke strong nations afar off; and they shall beat their swords into plough shares, and their spears into pruninghooks: nation shall not lift up a sword against nation, neither shall they learn war anymore."

Chapter 8

Rejecting the False Promise of War

The Failure of Peace Through Force

In the previous chapters, we explored how the Golden Rule serves as a framework for Peace and how Jesus' vision confronts the deep structural violence faced by the vulnerable. Now, we turn to one of humanity's longest-standing beliefs, the idea that war, or the use of superior firepower, can establish lasting Peace.

For millennia, civilisations, nations and societies have operated on the assumption that violence can bring about Peace, that the threat or use of overwhelming force or intimidation to bring compliance is the most effective way to uphold law and order, to secure harmony, prosperity, and stability. From the ancient empires to modern superpowers, the concept of "Peace through strength" has dominated the global landscape. This is a false premise, one that has led to untold suffering, destruction, and cycles of violence and war that continue to this very day, ever present before our very eyes.

In contrast, Jesus authors an entirely different vision: a Peace not achieved by violence, domination, or fear, but by reconciliation, justice, and self-sacrificial love. This Peace is not only a cessation of war and conflict but the presence of God's kingdom, where hearts are transformed, relationships restored, where progress and growth are encouraged. In this chapter, we will look into the historical failure of war as a means to Peace and how Jesus' message calls us to reject the false promises of war in favour of a true Peace found in His kingdom residing in our hearts and diadem to conscience.

The Historical Failure of Peace by Superior Firepower

Throughout history, we have witnessed countless examples of nations and empires rising and falling by the sword. From the Roman Empire, which sought to impose Peace across the Mediterranean through conquest and domination, to the World Wars of the 20th century, which promised a lasting Peace through the defeat of enemies, humanity has repeatedly turned to violence in the hope of creating a stable and prosperous world.

However, these efforts have repeatedly proven futile. Every victory achieved by force inevitably sows the seeds of the next conflict. The Roman Empire, for all its grandeur, eventually crumbled under the weight of its own violence. The Treaty of Versailles, intended to bring Peace after World War I, instead paved the way for World War II by humiliating and alienating the defeated nations. And in modern times, wars fought in the name of security, freedom, and democracy, often leave behind a legacy of instability and resentment.

At the heart of this failure is the simple truth that violence breeds more violence. Matthew 26:52 records Jesus saying, "Put your sword back in its place... for all who draw the sword will die by the sword." This timeless warning reminds us what goes around, comes around, that violence only perpetuates the very conflicts it seeks to resolve. The cycle of war and retaliation traps humanity in a never-ending loop of destruction, leaving lasting scars on societies, the devastation of homes and families, and broken individuals.

The Cold War offers another stark example of the futility of peace through superior firepower, which tends to bring forward an attitude of life unto the death, rather than a life unto life attitude or spirit. For decades, the world lived under the shadow of mutually assured destruction, with the superpowers of the United States and the Soviet Union amassing nuclear weapons capable of destroying all life on Earth. Though direct conflict was avoided, the constant threat of annihilation created an atmosphere of fear and division, not Peace. Even today, we live with the consequences of this arms race, as nuclear proliferation continues to pose a grave threat, to global stability under pressure from climate crises.

Jesus' Teachings
on Non-violence and Peace

In stark contrast to the world's approach to Peace through force, Jesus taught and lived a message of non-violence and Peace through reconnecting, and restoring unity of Spirit. In the Sermon on the Mount, Jesus makes it clear His kingdom operates on entirely different principles from those of the world. Romans 12:2 says, be not conformed to this world: but be ye transformed by the renewing of your mind, that ye may prove what is that good, and acceptable, and perfect, will of God. Paul, along with Jesus is not simply advocating for the absence of conflict; Jesus is calling for a proactive pursuit of Peace, one that seeks to heal divisions and restore relationships.

Jesus' own life is the ultimate demonstration of non-violent resistance. When faced with arrest, suffering, and death, He did not fight back or call on His followers to take up arms in His defence. In Matthew 26:53-54, when Peter draws his sword to protect Jesus, Jesus rebukes him, saying, "Do you think I cannot call on my Father, and He will at once put at my disposal more than twelve legions of angels? But how then would the Scriptures be fulfilled that say it must happen in this way?"

Jesus had the power to defend Himself with overwhelming force, yet He chose the path of non-violence, willingly laying down His life on the cross to achieve a Peace that transcends human understanding or total comprehension. In doing so, Jesus shows us that true Peace is not won in battle through the destruction of enemies but through the sacrifice of self, the laying down of one's life for the sake of others. As described in Ephesians 6:12-20, new truths can take care of outdated cultural traditions and high held doctrines of the past.

This vision of Peace stands in sharp contrast to the world's ways. Luke 6:27-29 further underscores this entirely better approach: "But to you who are listening I say: Love your enemies, do good to those who hate you, bless those who curse you, pray for those who mistreat you. If someone slaps you on one cheek, turn to them the other also." Here, Jesus calls His followers to love, forgiveness, and humility, even in the face of violence and aggression. Peace is an active, courageous commitment to reject the traditional cycle of violence under the auspices of peace by superior firepower and embrace the more transformative power of God's love, bringing forth new truth for our salvation.

The Cost of Violence
on the Soul of Humanity

The toll that violence takes on humanity is not only physical, but spiritual. War leaves behind more than destroyed cities and broken bodies; it shatters the human spirit, corrupting the image of God within us. Soldiers who return from battle often bear the scars of moral injury, having been forced to take lives in the name of Peace. Civilians caught in the crossfire live with the trauma of loss and fear. Entire generations are shaped by the violence they witness and endure, perpetuating the cycle of hatred and revenge.

In Matthew 5:38-39, Jesus addresses the natural human desire for retribution, saying, "You have heard that it was said, 'Eye for eye, and tooth for tooth.' But I tell you, do not resist an evil person. If anyone slaps you on the right cheek, turn to them the other cheek also." This teaching shakes the very foundations of human justice, which often seeks to balance the scales of justice through punishment, revenge, or retribution. Jesus calls us to something higher, a rejection of the belief violence can restore order, or balance the scales of justice.

Instead, Jesus offers the Peace of forgiveness and reconciliation, a Peace that heals the wounds of violence rather than deepening them. The spiritual cost of war is the loss of our capacity for mercy, compassion, and love, the very attributes that reflect God's image in us. War hardens hearts, dehumanizes enemies, numbs our souls, and sears our conscience to the suffering of others. Jesus' teachings remind us that the true victory is not in the defeat of our enemies but in the transformation of our hearts, where friendships are formed instead.

Embracing Non-violence as Jesus Taught

To embrace the Peace that Jesus offers, we must make the difficult choice to reject violence in all of its forms. This does not mean ignoring injustice or failing to stand up for the oppressed, but it does mean choosing to confront evil with non-violent resistance and better truths. The life of Martin Luther King Jr. offers a modern example of this principle in action. Inspired by Jesus' teachings, Dr King was lead to a movement for civil rights that rejected violence, even in the face of overwhelming brutal opposition. He believed that non-violence was not only the most ethical approach but the most effective one, as it exposed the injustice of the oppressor while preserving the dignity of the oppressed.

Jesus calls us to love our enemies and to seek their redemption, not their destruction. This Peace approach to conflict challenges the very core of our instincts, yet it is the only way to break the cycle of violence and create lasting Peace. Romans 12:21 urges us, "Do not be overcome by evil, but overcome evil with good." This verse encapsulates the essence of Jesus' non-violent approach: rather than allowing evil to dictate our actions, we are called to be kind and respond with goodness, mercy, and grace.

Practical Applications:

Remaining in Peace:

Remaining in Peace means trusting that Jesus' way of non-violence and love is more powerful than the world's methods of force and domination. It requires daily surrender to God's way and a commitment to living out His Peace in every situation. When faced with conflict, ask yourself: How can I respond with Peace instead of force? Make it a habit to pause before reacting, allowing the Holy Spirit to guide you toward a Peaceful resolution.

Living in Peace:

Living in Peace involves rejecting the instinct to retaliate or seek revenge when wronged. Instead, it means embracing forgiveness, accepting the consequences of someone else's mistakes, and seeking reconciliation and reunification of endeavour. Reflect on Matthew 5:9 and Romans 12:18 where both remind us of the importance of being Peacemakers in a world that often chooses violence as a means to peace. In your relationships, practice active listening, empathy, and kindness, and strive to resolve conflict through dialogue and understanding rather than confrontation.

Walking with His Peace:

Walking with His Peace requires a commitment to living out the values, of the kingdom of God being within us, every day. This means rejecting violence outright, not only in physical actions, but also in our thoughts, words, and attitudes. Ask God to transform your heart and renew your mind so you can become a vessel of His Peace in every interaction. Isaiah 2:4 speaks of a time when nations will beat their swords into ploughshares and no longer learn war anymore. May this vision of Peace shape the way you live and engage in the world around you.

Summary:

To conclude this chapter, we have examined the failure of war as a way or means of achieving Peace, and the radical alternative Jesus has on offer, a Peace created in love, kindness, non-violence, reconciliation, and grace. To follow Jesus is to reject the false promise of war and embrace the true Peace found only in self-sacrificial love and non-violent resistance. To reiterate, His Peace is not passive but actively seeks to transform hearts, renew minds, heal divisions, and break cycles of violence that have plagued humanity for far too long. This chapter is a timely reminder to stay in the better tree of progress and out of the quagmire of stagnation, trying to decide right from wrong in our own understanding. In the next chapter, Chapter 9: Kindness is Peace in Action, we will deep dive into how Peace is not merely a concept but something that is lived out in everyday acts of kindness. We will look at how the Spirit of Peace moves through our actions, using kindness to foster unity and reconciliation, to heal relationships, and rebuild communities of Peace. We'll see that Peace, when put into action, becomes a powerful force for transformation in our personal lives and in the world all around.

❖⟫⟫⟫-⟪⟪⟪❖

Recommended Bible Reading:

Matthew 26:47-56 –Jesus Rebukes Peter's Use of the Sword

This passage recounts Jesus' arrest in the Garden of Gethsemane, where Peter, in an attempt to defend Jesus, draws his sword and strikes the servant of the high priest. Jesus immediately rebukes Peter and tells him to put away his sword, declaring, "For all who draw the sword will die by the sword." This moment is a powerful demonstration of Jesus' rejection of violence and His commitment to fulfilling His mission of Peace through self-sacrifice.

Acts 9:1-19 –The Conversion of Saul (Paul)

Saul, a violent persecutor of Christians, encounters Jesus on the road to Damascus and is totally transformed. This story shows the power of Jesus' Peace to turn a heart bent on violence into one committed to spreading the gospel of the grace of God, the good news of Jesus' kingdom of Peace. Saul's conversion reminds us that even the most hardened hearts can be transformed by the gospel of Peace, showing that Peace is not about overpowering our enemies with force but more about transforming them with the power of the love of God.

Matthew 7:22-23 –Jesus warns us

Jesus warns us not to race ahead without Him and to stay in the fold.

Group Study Questions

1. How has history shown the failure of war to create lasting Peace, and what can we learn from these failures?

2. What does Jesus' example of non-violence teach us about confronting injustice without resorting to violence?

3. In what ways does violence affect the soul of humanity, and how can the Peace of Christ bring healing?

4. How can we apply the teachings of Jesus on non-violence and Peace in our modern world, both in personal conflicts and on a larger societal scale?

5. How does John 15:12-13 influence the way we look back over history?

A Process of Considerations Forward

PURPOSE ☺

HELP

Open to Suggestion

Resolving

Incorporate

Action

Establish

Decision

Considers Judgement Right & Wrong

Choice

Enter HOPE Consider BETTER

Direction

Entrench

Opinion

Separate

Considering

Closed to Suggestion

HARM

Here & Now
ACCEPTANCE
Only Time can tell

Clear Choice
Right, Wrong or Better?
Choosing better is choosing wisely

Moving forward through the process of consideration. Help is better than harm when a smile is the desired destination.

Chapter 9

Kindness is Peace in Action

From Rejecting War to Embracing Peace Through Action

In Chapter 8, we examined the false promise of war and violence, rejecting the idea Peace can be achieved through fear of harm or force. We saw how Jesus calls us to an entirely different way of non-violence, love, and unity of endeavour. Now, in this chapter, we turn our attention to how Peace can be lived out in the world. Peace, as taught by Jesus, is not a passive state of being, but something active, embodied in our thoughts, words, actions, and heart's desire.

One of the most powerful ways we manifest the Peace of Christ is through charity of kindness. The smallest acts of compassion, when done in love, ripple outward, creating Peace in our relationships, communities, and the broader world around us. Kindness, empowered by the Holy Spirit, is the tangible expression of Peace in action. Through kindness and generosity of Spirit, we become agents of Peace and charity, bringing healing, reconciliation, and grace, to those around us.

In this chapter, we will explore how the Spirit of Peace works through us, guiding us to embody Peace through everyday acts of kindness, generosity, and love. We will see that, as followers of Christ, we are called to be vessels of His Peace and to be demonstrating His kingdom through our interactions with the wider world.

How Kindness Brings Peace into Being

The fruit of the Spirit, love, joy, Peace, patience, kindness, goodness, faithfulness, gentleness, honesty and self-control, reveals the characteristics of a life lived in the Spirit (Galatians 5:22-23). Among these, kindness is one of the most visible and practical ways we can bring Peace into the world. Kindness is the language of Peace as it softens hearts, builds bridges, renders a smile, and creates a safety where reconciliation, empathy, and understanding can flourish.

When we engage in acts of kindness, we break down the walls of hostility and division that often separate people. A kind word spoken in love can defuse tension, heal a wounded heart, or restore a broken relationship. Ephesians 4:29 reminds us, "Speak words that are helpful and bring grace to others." Kindness is a disarming force, one which can transform frustration and struggles into genuine dialogue, and resentment into caring empathy.

Jesus Himself modelled this throughout His ministry. He was constantly reaching out to those on the margins of society. To the sick, the poor, the outcasts, the naughty, and the sinners. His acts of kindness, from healing the blind to forgiving the sinful, were not only miraculous but also profoundly Peaceable. By offering compassion, care, understanding and acceptance, Jesus showed kindness as His powerful agent for Peace.

In the story of the Good Samaritan (Luke 10:25-37), Jesus

illustrates the transformative power of kindness. A man is beaten, robbed, and left for dead on the side of the road. While a priest and a Levite pass by, it is the Samaritan, an outsider, traditionally despised by the Jews, who stops and shows compassion. He bandages the man's wounds, takes him to an inn, and pays for his care. The Samaritan's act of kindness not only saves the man's life but also breaks down the barriers of enmity between their two peoples. Jesus' message is clear, kindness knows no boundaries, and it is through such actions that we implant and establish Peace as the kingdom of God.

The Power of Small Acts of Compassion

It is easy to underestimate the power of small acts of kindness. In a world that often glorifies grand gestures and monumental achievements, we may feel our small efforts to be kind are insignificant. However, Jesus teaches us that the kingdom of Peace operates differently. In Matthew 25:35-40, Jesus says even the smallest acts, such as feeding the hungry, giving a drink to the thirsty, welcoming the stranger, are all significant in the eyes of God. Whatever you did for one of the least of these brothers and sisters of mine, you did for me.

The small, daily acts of compassion we offer up, helping a neighbour out, taking time to listen to someone in need, showing patience with a difficult or troubling person, all of these are powerful acts of Peace. These actions may seem small in isolation, but they accumulate over time, cultivating a culture of Peace in our homes, groups, schools, workplaces, communities, tribes, and nations. Just as a pebble creates ripples when dropped into a pond, so to do our acts of kindness send ripples of Peace into the world around us.

The Spirit of Peace moves through these seemingly ordinary

moments. When we allow the Holy Spirit to guide our words and actions, we become instruments of His Peace. Through our kindness, we reflect the heart, the face, and the hands of God, inviting others to experience His Peace in their lives. Colossians 3:12 says to us, "Therefore, as God's chosen people, holy and dearly loved, clothe yourselves with compassion, care, kindness, humility, gentleness, and patience."

Transforming Relationships and Communities Through Kindness

Kindness has the power not only to transform individuals but also to rebuild relationships and reshape communities. Conflict, division, and resentment often tear at the fabric of our relationships, whether within families, friendships, workplaces, or communities. But kindness, when practiced consistently, begins to heal wounds, and restore trust.

In Romans 12:20-21, Paul encourages believers to overcome evil with good, saying, "If your enemy is hungry, feed him; if he is thirsty, give him something to drink. In doing this, you will heap burning coals on his head. Do not be overcome by evil, but overcome evil with good." Here, we see that kindness toward our enemies has the power to break the cycle of conflict and retaliation. It disarms hostility and invites the possibility of reconciliation.

Imagine a community where kindness is the prevailing value. Instead of gossip, competition, or judgment, neighbours look out for one another, support each other in times of need, and offer help without expecting anything in return. Such a community would reflect the Peace of God's kingdom on earth, demonstrating that kindness is a practical, powerful force for building a better world for all to enjoy, all the more.

Peace in Action:
Living Out the Golden Rule Daily

At the heart of Jesus' teachings is the Golden Rule: "So in everything you do, do to others equally what you would have them be fairly doing to you" (Matthew 7:12). This simple yet profound command encapsulates the essence of Peace in action. The Golden Rule challenges us to treat others with the same love, compassion, respect, and kindness that we desire for ourselves. It is the foundation of kind thinking, calling us to step outside of ourselves and consider the needs and well-being of others.

Living out the Golden Rule daily requires intentionality. It means being mindful of our interactions and seeking opportunities to show more kindness, even when it is inconvenient or difficult. Whether we are dealing with a family member, a colleague, or a stranger, the Golden Rule reminds us to act with empathy, always considering how we can bring Peace to any situation.

Philippians 2:3-4 encourages us to "do nothing out of selfish ambition or vain conceit. Rather, in humility value others above yourselves, not looking to your own interests but each of you to the interests of others." When we live with this mindset, kindness becomes a natural expression of our faith, and Peace flows out toward other people through our kind actions.

Summary:

In summary, in this chapter we have explored how kindness serves as the practical expression of Peace in our lives. By engaging in small acts of compassion and living out the Golden Rule, we become agents of Peace, transforming us as well as our relationships and communities. Kindness, guided by the Spirit of Truth, breaks down walls and barriers, heals wounds and animosities, and creates a vibrant culture of care reflecting His Kingdom called Peace.

In Chapter 10: Education Over Coercion, we will examine how example, rather than force, can be used as a tool for spreading Peace and grace. We will explore how teaching, demonstrating, exampling, encouraging, instructing, mentoring, guiding or coaching others with love, truth, and understanding create a more lasting and transformative Peace than does the use of power, strength, fear, or control.

Practical Applications:
Remaining in Peace:

Remaining in Peace means cultivating a mindset of kindness. Each day, look for opportunities to be kind, even in small ways. When troubles arise, ask yourself, "How can I respond with kindness rather than anger or frustration?" By choosing kindness, you not only remain calm in Peace but also bring Peace into the lives of others. Reflect on Galatians 5:22-23 as a guide, letting the fruit of the Spirit, especially kindness, guide your actions.

Living in Peace:

Living in Peace involves making kindness and generosity a consistent practice. It is not about grand gestures but about the small, daily acts of compassion that build relationships and foster trust. Consider how you can make kindness and generosity a habit within your family home, workplace, amongst friends and within your community. Make an effort to listen carefully to other people, offering a helping hand, or speaking words of encouragement. In doing this, you create spaces of Peace and grace wherever you go.

Walking with His Peace:

Walking with His Peace means carrying kindness with you as a way of life. Whether you are interacting with strangers or loved ones, always seek to embody the Peace of Christ through your actions. Walking with His Peace is an ongoing journey toward becoming more like Christ and allowing His kindness to flow through you into every situation. Ephesians 4:32 reminds us to "be kind and compassionate to one another, forgiving each other, just as in Christ God forgave you."

Group Study Questions

1. How does kindness serve as an active expression of Peace in your daily life?
2. What are some small acts of compassion that you can incorporate into your routine to foster Peace in your relationships?
3. How can Peace prevent opportunism without destroying opportunity?
4. How can you foster more Peace?
5. Joke: Why does Jesus eat at Japanese restaurants? Because He loves Miso

Recommended Bible Reading:
Matthew 8:1-4 –The Healing of the Leper

In this story, Jesus encounters a man with leprosy, an outcast in society due to his illness. Instead of avoiding him, Jesus reaches out and touches the man, healing him. This act of kindness not only restores the man's health but also his dignity, demonstrating how compassion brings healing and Peace to those who are marginalized.

Ruth 2-4 –The Story of Ruth and Boaz

The relationship between Ruth and Boaz is a beautiful example of kindness leading to Peace. Boaz shows kindness to Ruth, a foreign widow, by providing for her and protecting her. His compassion transforms her circumstances, leading to a relationship that brings healing and restoration not only to Ruth, but also to her family. Boaz's kindness is a reflection of God's heart for the vulnerable, demonstrating how acts of compassion can transform lives and bring Peace into broken situations.

Acts 15 –Bride leaves the groom

In Acts 15, man replaces God's authority with a council, shifting from grace to works. Council attempts to mix God's free gift of grace with human prescriptions of holiness, diminishing the power of Christ's blood. This brings harm and hurt instead of healing and restoration.

In verse 28, the bride departs from the groom. Yet we are not to fear, or despair, for salvation remains at hand. Council could have repeated the words of Jesus when He said, "Only God is Holy, you know life's rules, don't lie, cheat, rob, steal, or kill. Love God, respect your parents, and care for other people. Putting self aside, treat people the way you would want people to fairly treat you. This is my commandment, the law, and the prophets. (Matthew 7;12, Mark 10: 18-19, Luke 6;27, John 15: 12-13)

By the chapter's end, division amongst church leadership, and the varying brands start to take hold in the church, revealing the consequences of straying from Christ's perfect Peace and grace.

Chapter 10

Education Over Coercion

The Power of Influence Over Control

In Chapter 9, we looked at how kindness serves as a powerful expression of Peace in action. Now, we turn to another vital aspect of Jesus' approach, an emphasis on education and guidance rather than harm, force, duress, or coercion. Jesus' method was never to force His followers into submission or compliance, but to teach, lead by example, introduce new truths, and nurture them through love and understanding.

In our world today, coercion often seems to be the quickest way to resolve conflict, maintain order, or achieve a desired result. From politics to education to family life, the temptation to use force, whether physical, emotional, or intellectual persists. However, using coercion, while seemingly effective in the short term, often leads to resentment, rebellion, and division in the long term. In contrast, education in new truths offers us a path to sustainable Peace by transforming hearts and minds from within.

Jesus demonstrated the best way to bring about lasting change is through patient teaching, modelling honest behaviour, authenticity, and cultivating a much deeper understanding of God's will. This chapter will explore how education, both spiritual and practical, can build stronger, kinder, more Peaceable communities and relationships by empowering progress and growth in people to learn, and choose Peace on their own terms

Why Force Escalates Conflict

The compulsive use of force, or fear of harm, whether in a family setting, our workplaces, or on a larger civic scale, tends to escalate conflict rather than resolve it. Force imposes compliance but rarely changes hearts. When people feel coerced or bullied, they may outwardly comply, but often will harbour resentment, anger, or a desire for revenge. This is especially true when force is used to maintain or suppress dissent.

In Matthew 20:25-28, Jesus highlights the difference between worldly authority, which often relies on force, and the servant leadership He calls His followers to adopt; "You know the rulers of the Gentiles lord it over them, and their high officials exercise authority over them. Not so with you. Instead, whoever wants to become great among you must be your servant, and whoever wants to be first must be your slave, just as the Son of Man did not come to be served, but to serve, and to give His life as a ransom for many."

Here, Jesus points out that true leadership is about service, not dominance. When we try to exert control over others through coercive means, we will fail to lead them toward true growth, transformation, or Peace. Instead, we create environments of bitterness, fear, resentment, and division, which often lead to deeper conflict. In contrast, education in new truths through genuine, transparent, and compassionate leadership, encourages better growth in individuals, more understanding and better cooperation amongst colleagues, and responses to the wisdom of Peace.

Jesus' Teachings on Leading by Example

Jesus consistently modelled leading by example rather than through force. He never forced His disciples to follow Him or adhere to His teachings, but instead offered them the truth, trusting they would come to understand and embrace His way in time. Jesus' approach to leadership is most vividly seen in how He served others. Laying down His life and dying on the cross. Washing His disciples' feet, feeding the hungry, healing the sick, protecting the children, and teaching the multitudes with patience and love.

In John 13:12-17, after washing His disciples' feet, Jesus says, "Now that I, your Lord and Teacher, have washed your feet, you also should wash each other's feet. I have set you an example that you should do as I have done for you." This act of humility and service speaks volumes about the kind of leadership Jesus embodied. He didn't impose His will on others; instead, He invited them to follow His example of selfless, sacrificial love and service.

By leading with humility, Jesus showed His disciples that real authority comes from serving others, not by lording it over or dominating them. He transformed the traditional understanding of power and authority, teaching that true strength lies in the ability to lift others up, educate them, and lead them to discover new truths for themselves.

This method, of education over coercion, is more effective because it allows individuals to internalise what they've learned and applying it with genuine understanding, rather than out of fear or obligation. When people are taught with compassion and respect, they are far more likely to embrace the values of Peace, love, and justice, and to carry those values forward in their own lives.

The Role of Education in Spreading Peace

Education plays a crucial role in spreading Peace, both on a personal level and within communities. The ability to teach others about Peace, conflict resolution, and mutual respect, is foundational to creating lasting change.

When we educate others, we plant the seeds of Peace in their hearts and minds, encouraging people to invite Jesus into their heart and conscience, helping them to develop the skills and understanding needed to foster Peace in their own Spirit, relationships, and communities.

Education equips people with the tools to think critically, solve problems, and approach conflict with wisdom and compassion. Education can encourage dialogue and open-mindedness, which are essential for overcoming the divisions that so often lead to violence and conflict.

By educating people about the Gospel of Peace, we help them to see the world through the lens of God's love and justice, rather than through eyes of fear, hatred, or power struggles.

Consider the parable of the sower in Matthew 13:1-23, where Jesus teaches about the different types of soil that represent the hearts of people who hear His word. Those who receive the word in good soil, who are open to learning, growth, and change, are able to produce a great harvest. Similarly, when we educate others with love and patience, we provide the fertile ground for Peace to take root and flourish.

Teaching others about the principles of Peace and grace, including truth telling, kindness, forgiveness, nonviolent resistance, love, and reconciliation, can transform societies and civility from the ground up.

Just as Jesus' teachings have shaped the course of history, so too can our efforts to educate others about Peace and empathy help to shape a future where conflicts are resolved through understanding and wisdom rather than force and harm. We can learn war no more and instead, learn to live at peace, in Peace, with His Peace.

Building a Culture of Learning and Growth

In order to foster lasting Peace, we must create a culture of learning and growth in excellence. Both in our personal lives and in our communities. A culture of lifelong learning values dialogue, curiosity, and respect, honouring a diversity of perspectives. The more perspectives, the greater our understanding of others can be. The broader our comprehension will become.

It encourages individuals to ask questions, seek understanding, and grow in wisdom. This is the kind of culture Jesus fostered among His disciples, where they were free to ask questions, express any doubts, and learn more from His example, knowledge and experience.

In today's world, a culture of learning can help bridge divides of right from wrong and heal wounds caused by prejudice, discrimination, unconscious bias, fear of the different, misinformation, and misunderstanding.

By promoting education over coercion, we empower individuals to engage with one another in meaningful dialogue, shared experiences, listen to alternative perspectives, empathise, and find common ground or goals. This approach fosters mutual benefit, respect, cooperation, and coexistence, which are essential for building more peaceable communities.

One of the most effective ways to build a culture of learning is through sharing experiences, mentorship, coaching, and discipleship. Jesus spent three years walking alongside His disciples, teaching them not only through His words but also through His actions. He modelled compassion, care, humility, and servant leadership, guiding them toward a deeper, clearer, more intensive understanding of God's kingdom.

As followers of Christ, we are called to do the same, mentoring others in the ways of Peace, guiding them with patience and love, and empowering them to become citizens of Peace in their own right.

In Proverbs 22:6, we are reminded of the long-lasting impact of teaching; "Start children off on the way they should go, and even when they are old, they will not depart or turn from it." While this verse speaks of the importance of early instruction, its message applies to people of all ages. Education, rooted in love, transparency, mutual benefit, and respect, lays the foundation for a lifetime of security, authenticity, and peaceful living, prosperous, open minded, and profitable, growing in new truths, and excellence.

Jesus' Teachings on Leading by Example, Not Force

Jesus consistently led by example, demonstrating that education, and mentoring are more effective than bullying. His life exemplified the power of non-coercive leadership, one that invites others to follow willingly, rather than through compulsion, force, or obligation. Throughout the Gospels, we see Jesus engaging with people through teaching, coaching dialogue, and demonstration, rather than through bullying, force, or coercion.

In Matthew 11:29, Jesus invites us to "Take my yoke upon you and learn from me, for I am gentle and humble in heart, and you will find rest for your souls." Jesus' method of teaching was one of gentleness and patience, not pressure or intimidation. He invited people to learn from Him because He knew that true transformation comes not from force but through relationship, from walking alongside someone and showing them a better way to go, even to find their own new truths, and then, to walk along with others.

This kind of leadership is far more effective in creating lasting Peace because it empowers individuals to make choices based on their own understanding and convictions, rather than out of fear. Jesus didn't force anyone to follow Him, but His example of Peace, love, mercy, and grace drew people to Him as well as changed their lives for the better. Similarly, when we lead others through education in new truths, and encouragement, delivering example, we invite them to discover the Peace of Heaven for themselves.

Summary:

In summary, we have examined how education, rather than coercion, offers a better way forward in spreading Peace, unity, kindness, and harmony, which is transformative to hearts and minds. Through kind teaching, leading by example, and building a culture of learning, we empower others to internalise the values of Peace, non-violent resistance instead of rebellion, kind heartedness, restoring reconciliation, truth, and honesty.

Jesus' method of non-coercive leadership shows us that true and lasting change comes from a discovery within, not from outward force or pressure applied, as Hebrews Chapter five explains, in the Order of Melchizedek, King and High Priest of Peace.

In Chapter 11: The Return of Christ and Perfected Kingdom of Peace, we will turn our attention to the prophetic vision of Christ's return and completion of His kingdom of Peace here on earth. We will explore how this vision fulfils the promises of Scripture and what it means for us as we live in the hope of His coming reign, where Peace will be fully realized, and all things will be made new.

Practical Applications:

Remaining in Peace:

Remaining in Peace involves continually seeking wisdom and understanding. Make it a daily habit to learn, through Scripture, prayer, and reflection, how you can better live out the teachings of Jesus. As you grow in knowledge and understanding of God, you will find that Peace can become more deeply rooted in your life. Reflect on Proverbs 4:5-7; "Get wisdom, get understanding: forget it not; forsake her not, and she shall preserve thee: love her, and she shall keep thee. Wisdom is the principal thing; therefore get wisdom: and with all thy getting get understanding."

Living in Peace:

Living in Peace means actively choosing education over coercion in your interactions with others. Whether in your family, groups, workplace, or community, seek to teach and guide through example, love, patience, and understanding rather than through demand, force, or control. As Colossians 3:16 encourages, "Let the message of Christ dwell among you richly as you teach and admonish one another with all wisdom." By prioritizing education, you foster an environment where Peace can flourish.

Walking with His Peace:

Walking with His Peace requires us to be examples of Christ's love in action. In your daily walk, strive to lead by example, showing others what it means to live in Peace through your actions, words, and attitudes. Let the Holy Spirit guide you in how to mentor, teach, and encourage others on their journey toward Peace. Ephesians 4:29 reminds us, "Do not let any unwholesome talk come out of your mouths, but only what is helpful for building others up according to their needs, that it may benefit those who listen."

⊹❋⊱⊰❋⊹

Recommended Bible Reading:
John 3:1-21 –Jesus Teaches Nicodemus

In this passage, Jesus engages in a deep conversation with Nicodemus, a Pharisee, explaining the concept of being "born again" and the spiritual truths of the kingdom of God and Spirit named by Jesus as Peace. Rather than bullying Nicodemus into belief, Jesus teaches him with patience and wisdom, allowing him to come to an understanding of the truth at his own pace. This story exemplifies Jesus' educational approach to spreading the Gospel of Peace.

2 Timothy 1:1-7 –Paul and Timothy: A Mentoring Relationship

The relationship between Paul and Timothy illustrates the power of coaching in spreading the teachings of Christ. Paul's letters to Timothy offer encouragement, guidance, and wisdom, empowering Timothy to lead and teach others with confidence. This story reflects how education and applied mentorship can and will strengthen individuals to become leaders and agents of Peace in their own communities.

Group Study Questions

1. Joke: Why is Jesus not in a formal relationship? Because He's still hung up on His X.
2. How can we build a culture of learning and growth in our own communities that fosters Peace and understanding?
3. Joke: Why does Jesus wash His Apostle's feet? So

He can cleanse their soles.

4. In what ways can mentorship and discipleship play a role in spreading the message of Peace?
5. How might you think about coaching a friend?

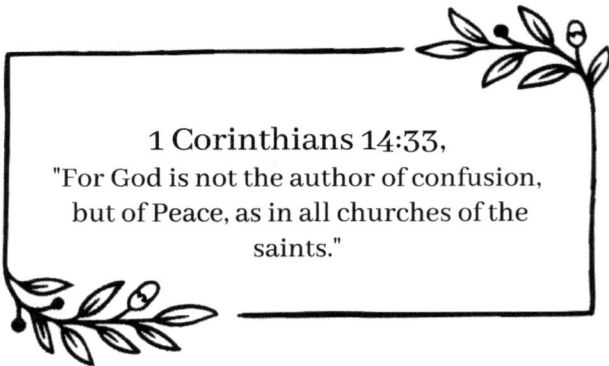

> ### 1 Corinthians 14:33,
> "For God is not the author of confusion, but of Peace, as in all churches of the saints."

Chapter 11

Jesus Perfects His Kingdom of Peace

The Prophetic Vision of Jesus' Return

Throughout the Bible, we find countless promises of the coming kingdom of God, a time when all things will be made new and the world will be fully restored under the reign of Jesus Christ. As believers, we live in the tension between the "already" and the "not yet," the kingdom of God has already been inaugurated through the life, death, and resurrection of Christ, but its complete fulfilment will only come when He returns. This return of Christ is the moment when God's ultimate plan for Peace, justice, and restoration will be realized.

In previous chapters, we've explored how we are called to live out Peace in our lives, relationships, workplaces, and communities. Now, we shift our focus to the culmination of all these efforts, the return of Christ, along with His perfected kingdom of Peace and put an end to all violence, suffering, and injustice. This chapter will take us through the biblical promises of Jesus' return and the significance of this future hope for believers today.

Jesus as the King of Peace

One of the key aspects of Jesus' identity is that He is the Prince of Peace. In Isaiah 9:6-7, the prophet declares, "For to us a child is born, to us a son is given, and the government will be on his shoulders. And he will be called Wonderful Counsellor, Mighty God, Everlasting Father, Prince of Peace. Of the greatness of His government and Peace there will be no end." This prophecy, spoken centuries before the birth of Christ, points to Jesus as the one who will establish a government of Peace, one that will never end.

Jesus' first coming initiated the kingdom of Peace, and His second coming will bring it to completion. During His earthly ministry, Jesus often spoke of the kingdom of God, a kingdom marked by love, justice, and Peace. However, we still live in a world marred by sin, conflict, and war. The return of Christ is the promise that one day, all things will be perfected, and His kingdom of Peace will be fully accomplished on Earth.

In Revelation 19:11-16, we see a vision of Christ returning as a victorious king, riding on a white horse, with the title "King of kings and Lord of lords." This image of Christ's triumphant return is one of justice and restoration. He comes not to bring destruction, but to defeat evil and perfect a reign of Peace and grace. The weapons of war will be turned into tools of creation and life as Jesus' reign as the King of Peace comes into being here on earth.

The Thousand-Year Reign of Peace and Justice

The millennium, a thousand-year reign of Christ on Earth, is another critical part of the biblical vision of Peace. In Revelation 20:1-6, John describes this reign of Peace and justice, where Satan is bound, and Christ rules over the

Earth with His saints. During this time, the world will experience an unprecedented era of Peace, free from the influence of evil and violence. The millennium represents a foretaste of the eternal Peace that will come when God makes all things new.

This thousand-year reign is often interpreted as a literal period of Peace on Earth, where Christ's rule will be characterised by justice, honesty, and harmony among all people. It will be a time of healing, where the divisions and conflicts that have torn humanity apart will be mended, and God's kingdom will flourish on Earth.

The prophet Micah also gives us a glimpse of this time in Micah 4:3-4, where he prophesies: "They will beat their swords into ploughshares and their spears into pruning hooks. Nation will not take up sword against nation, nor will they train for war anymore. Everyone will sit under their own vine and under their own fig tree, and no one will make them afraid, for the Lord Almighty has spoken." This beautiful imagery points to a world where weapons of war are transformed into tools for growth and provision, and where fear and violence are no more.

The millennium reminds us that Peace is not simply the absence of war but the presence of justice, honesty, and progress. It is a Peace that flows from God's perfect rule and the reconciliation of all things under Christ.

The Defeat of Satan and the Final Restoration

The Bible tells us that Christ's return will not only complete His kingdom of Peace but will also mark the final defeat of Satan, the enemy of Peace. In Revelation 20:7-10, we see that after the thousand-year reign, Satan will be released for a short time, but he will ultimately be defeated and thrown into the lake of fire, where he will no longer have any power to deceive or destroy.

This final defeat of Satan is the ultimate victory of Peace over evil. It signifies the end of all that corrupts and distorts God's creation, such as self-centredness, sin, death, violence, vanity, greed, prejudice, hatred, hypocrisy, and hindrance, to name but a few. With Satan's defeat, and our egos in line, the stage is set for the final restoration of all things. In Revelation 21:1-4, John sees a vision of the new heaven and the new earth, where God dwells with His people: "He will wipe every tear from their eyes. There will be no more death or mourning or crying or pain, for the old order of things has passed away."

This is the eternal kingdom of Peace. Jesus will fully develop and perfect, a place where all suffering and sorrow are gone, and God's people live in perfect harmony with Him and with one another. This is the fulfilment of God's promise of Peace, where every broken thing is made whole, and every wound is healed.

Living in the Hope of Jesus' Return

As believers, we are called to live in the hope of Jesus' return. This hope isn't without doing; it calls us to act, as our actions transform hope into faith, as we await the coming new heaven, Jesus' perfected kingdom of Peace. In 2 Peter 3:11-13, Peter reminds us, knowing the world will one day be renewed, to live honest and Godly lives as we look forward to the day of Perfection and speed its coming. Our lives can reflect the values of the kingdom we await, values of Peace, justice, love, joy, mercy, and grace.

While we wait for Christ's return, we are called to be ambassadors of His Peace on Earth. This means working to bring about Peace in our own lives, communities, and the world around us. It means living in such a way that our lives bear witness to the coming kingdom, showing others what it means to live under the reign of Jesus, King of Peace.

In Matthew 24:42-44, Jesus instructs His followers to "keep watch" and be ready for His return, for it will come at an hour

we do not expect. This call to vigilance is a reminder that we should live each day with the awareness Jesus Christ could come or return at any moment. Our anticipation of His coming kingdom should inspire us to live Peaceably, faithfully, and honestly, always seeking to advance His kingdom on Earth.

Practical Applications:

Remaining in Peace:

Remaining in Peace as we await Christ's return involves living with faith and hope in the promises of God. Even in times of uncertainty or conflict, we can remain grounded in the knowledge that since Easter, Jesus is now king of Peace and His perfected kingdom is coming soon. Spend time daily reflecting on the hope of Christ's return, 2 Peter 3:14 says, wherefore, beloved, seeing that ye look for such things, be diligent that ye may be found of Him in Peace, without spot, and blameless. Imagine shaking the hand of Jesus in person, and allowing this truth of His presence, to bring His Peace into your heart. Philippians 4:7 reminds us, "And the Peace of God, which transcends all understanding, will guard your hearts and your minds in Christ Jesus."

Living in Peace:

Living in Peace means actively working to bring about the values of the kingdom of Peace in your everyday life. This includes showing care, kindness, compassion, promoting justice, and seeking harmony in your relationships. Let your life be a reflection of the Peace Jesus promises, and let your actions point others toward the coming kingdom of God. Isaiah 26:3 encourages us, You will keep in perfect Peace those whose minds are steadfast, because they trust in you.

Walking with His Peace:

Walking with His Peace requires us to be ambassadors of Peace in a world that is often filled with turmoil, conflict, and division. As we await the return of Christ, we are called to walk and be found in His Peace at all times, demonstrating through our lives the transformative power of His love. (2 Peter 3:14) Pray for the Holy Spirit to guide you in being a Peacemaker, a cultural developer cultivating Peace culture, whether through small acts of kindness or larger efforts to promote Peace and justice. Ephesians 6:15 speaks of having our "feet fitted with the readiness that comes from the gospel of Peace." Let this readiness shape the way you walk and interact with the world, and broader community.

Summary:

To sum up this chapter, we've explored the prophetic vision of Christ's return and the physical perfecting of His kingdom of Peace here on Earth. This kingdom is characterized by justice, restoration, and the ultimate defeat of evil. As we live in the hope of this coming kingdom, we are called to be active participants in spreading Peace and preparing the world for Jesus' return.

In Chapter 12: Living in the Fullness of His Peace, we will dig into what it means to live in the fullness of Christ's Peace here and now, even as we await the completion of His kingdom to come. We will examine how the Holy Spirit empowers us to live as ambassadors, agents, and citizens of Peace here on earth and how we can cultivate a life of Peace, hope, and joy in the midst of a broken world.

Group Study Questions

1. Joke: Why did Jesus cross the road? He came back from the other side.

2. What does the Bible (Colossians 1:12-14) teach about God translating us into the Kingdom of His dear Son, Jesus Christ?

3. How does the millennium reflect God's plan for justice and restoration?

4. Joke: Why did Jesus give stilettos to all of the sick women? Because they wanted to be heeled.

❦❦❦

Recommended Bible Reading:

Matthew 25:1-13 –The Parable of the Ten Virgins

This parable emphasizes the importance of being prepared for the return of Christ. It reminds us that we must live in anticipation of His coming, always ready to welcome the King of Peace as we participate as citizens in His kingdom here on Earth.

Revelation 21:1-7 –The New Heaven and the New Earth

This passage offers a vision of the final restoration of Peace when God creates a new heaven and a new earth. It describes a world where God dwells among His people, and all suffering, death, and pain are wiped away. This vision of eternal Peace gives us hope and reminds us of the glorious future that awaits those already having Jesus in them. Word into flesh, Peace into being.

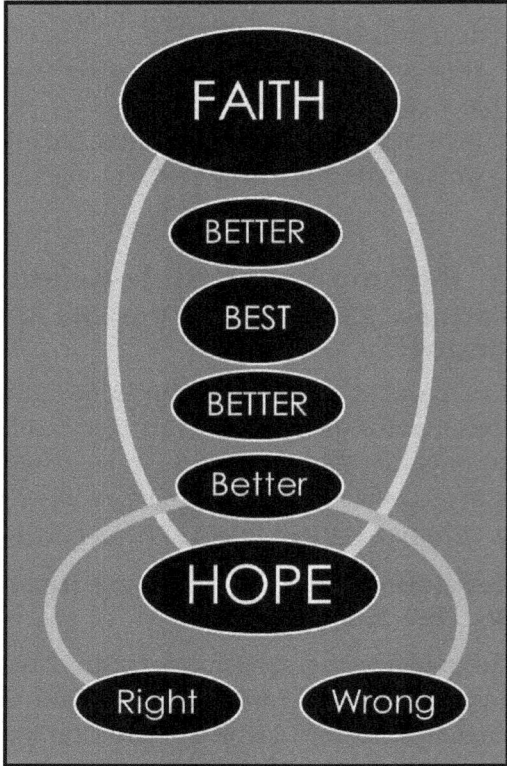

Always a better hope on offer, drawing us closer to God. Faith is the bringing into manifestation the evidence of things not seen, the substance of things hoped for.

Chapter 12

Living in the Fullness of His Peace

An Invitation to Embrace Jesus' Peace Now

In Chapter 11, we examined the prophetic vision of Jesus' return and the perfecting of His kingdom of Peace. That vision gave us hope for the future, but we don't have to wait until Christ's return to begin living in His Peace. Jesus offers us His Peace now, inviting us to experience the fullness of His Peace as we walk through life with Jesus in us.

This Peace isn't something abstract or unattainable. It's a present-day reality that flows from our relationship with Christ and the presence of the Holy Spirit within us. As followers of Christ, we are called to live in His Peace every day, letting it shape how we interact with other people, face challenges, maintain our sense of humour and inner calm trusting more in God's plan rather than our own understanding.

In this chapter, we will discover what it means to live in the fullness of His Peace, as citizens of Peace, and how we can embrace the Peace of Christ in every area of our lives. We will look at how the Holy Spirit empowers us to remain at Peace in difficult times, and how we can share this Peace with those around us, becoming ambassadors of Peace in a broken world.

The Role of the Holy Spirit in Establishing Peace Within Us

The Holy Spirit is the source of the Peace of Christ in our lives. When Jesus promised to send the Spirit of Truth to His followers, He described the Spirit as our Helper and Comforter. In John 16:7-15, Jesus says, "And when He is come, he will reprove the world of sin, and of righteousness, and of judgment: Of sin, because they believe not on me; Of righteousness, because I go to my Father, and ye see me no more; Of judgment, because the prince of this world is judged.

 I have yet many things to say unto you, but ye cannot bear them now. Howbeit when He, the Spirit of truth, is come, He will guide you into all truth: for He shall not speak of Himself; but whatsoever He shall hear, that shall He speak: and He will show you things to come. He shall glorify me: for He shall receive of mine, and shall shew it unto you. All things that the Father hath are mine: therefore said I, that He shall take of mine, and shall shew it unto you."

This Peace, which comes through the indwelling presence of the Spirit of Truth, is different from the fleeting peace that the world offers. Peace is more than a moment. It is a deep, abiding Peace that remains within us even in the midst of turmoil and trouble.

The Holy Spirit works within us to reprove our thinking and beliefs on sin, on righteousness and of judgement. This means as we grow in our relationship with Christ and allow the Holy Spirit to work in our lives, Peace becomes a natural outflow of our spiritual maturity.

Living in the fullness of His Peace, involves listening and surrendering to the guidance of the Holy Spirit. When we face stressful situations or conflict, it's easy to allow fear or anxiety to take over. But the Holy Spirit is there to remind us of God's promises, to calm our fears, and to fill us with the hope of God's Peace, which transcends all understanding.

2 Corinthians 13:11, suggests it's up to us now, be perfect, be of good comfort, be of one mind, live in the Spirit and kingdom of Peace; and the God of Peace, and love shall be with you. The more we lean on the Holy Spirit, the more we can experience the fullness of His Peace in every circumstance. We can learn to be at peace, in Peace, with His Peace.

Becoming Ambassadors of Peace in a World of Conflict

As followers of Christ, we are not only called into Peace to experience Peace for ourselves, but also to become special envoys of Peace in the world. This means that we are called to actively share the good news of Jesus' Kingdom of Peace and Jesus as the king of Peace with other people, helping to bring healing, restoration, and reconciliation to a flawed, broken, and overcrowded world filled with loneliness, sorrow, heartache, separation, pain, and unresolved conflict. 2 Corinthians 5:18-20 describes our role as ambassadors of reconciliation: "All this is from God, who reconciled us to himself through Christ and gave us the ministry of reconciliation... We are therefore Christ's ambassadors, as though God were making his appeal to the world through us."

As citizens of Peace, this means carrying the message of reconciliation and healing to those around us. It means forgiving those who have wronged us, helping to resolve conflicts, and bringing the love and Peace of Jesus into every circumstance. In a world where divisions and hostilities are common, the message of Christ's Peace is desperately needed. As His followers, we are called to be Peacemakers, working to bridge divides and promote unity, calm and harmony in our relationships, communities, and the world.

Jesus places a special blessing on those who actively pursue Peace and work to bring others into a place of reconciliation. Being a Peacemaker is not always easy, and it often requires us to lay down our pride or our desire for glory or honour. But when we choose the path of Peace, we reflect the heart of Christ and help to bring awareness to His kingdom here on earth.

Living in Hope of Jesus' Ultimate Return

Even as we live in the fullness of Christ's Peace today, we do so with the hope of His ultimate return. The Peace we experience now is but a foretaste of the complete and perfect Peace that will come when Jesus returns and establishes His Reign over all here on Earth. Romans 8:24-25 reminds us that "hope that is seen is no hope at all. Who hopes for what they already have? But if we hope for what we do not yet have, we wait for it patiently."

This hope, this better hope is what sustains us as we face the difficulties, the challenges, the suffering, the conflicts and struggles in the world. While we may not experience perfect Peace in every aspect of our lives right now, we hold on to the promise that one day, Christ will return to make all things new and better and His Peace will reign supreme forevermore, this hope empowers us to live with patience, faith, and endurance, knowing the fullness of His Peace is not far off.

Living in this hope also changes the way we approach our current circumstances. It reminds us the trials we face are temporary, and God's plan for Peace is unfolding. When we live in the fullness of His Peace, in the presence of Christ, we are able to trust in God's timing, assured His ultimate plan will bring about restoration and wholeness, both for us and for the world. A place without tears, war, or death.

Practical Applications:

Remaining in Peace:

To remain in Peace, cultivate a habit of daily prayer and reflection. Ask the Holy Spirit to fill you with Peace and guide you through life's challenges. Trust God is in control, and when anxiety arises, turn to Philippians 4:6-7, which encourages us to present our requests to God with thanksgiving, knowing that His Peace will guard our hearts and minds.

Living in Peace:

Living in Peace means actively pursuing restoration, reconciliation, and forgiveness in your relationships. When conflicts arise, seek to resolve them with grace, understanding, and wisdom. Let Peace be the guiding principle in your interactions with others, reflecting Christ's heart in all that you do.

Walking with His Peace:

Walking with His Peace means living out your faith in every situation, letting the Peace of Christ guide your actions, decisions, and responses. When faced with difficulties, remind yourself of John 14:27, where Jesus assures us that He gives us a miraculous Peace that the world can no way offer to us. As you go about your day, practice responding to challenges with calmness and trust, allowing God's Peace to permeate every area of your life. Remember to breathe and come back to the here and now. Be a witness to those around you, display your calmness, demonstrating the power of Peace in how you handle conflict, stress, and uncertainty.

Summary:

Concluding, the Holy Spirit empowers us to live in the fullness of Christ's Peace within us now, even as we look forward to the ultimate fulfilment of Peace when Jesus returns. We are called not only to experience Peace within ourselves but also to become sharing agents of His Peace, spreading His message of reconnection with the world, proclaiming the good news of His Peace.

In Chapter 13: The Universal Call to the Gospel of Peace, we will delve into how the gospel of Peace is a message for all of humanity. We will examine the mission to spread the good news of Christ's kingdom of Peace to all nations and how we, as followers of Christ, are called to carry this message to the ends of the earth.

Group Study Questions

1. How does the Holy Spirit empower us to live in the fullness of Christ's Peace today?
2. What does it mean to be an ambassador of Peace, and how can we share the Peace of Christ with others?
3. How does the hope of Jesus' return influence the way we experience Peace in our current circumstances?
4. In what ways can we actively cultivate a life of Peace, even in the midst of a broken and conflicted world?

❧⋙-⋘❧

Recommended Bible Reading:
Mark 4:35-41 –Jesus Calms the Storm

In this story, Jesus and His disciples are caught in a violent storm. While the disciples are filled with fear, Jesus remains at Peace, and with a word, He calms the storm. This story reminds us that Jesus brings Peace to our storms, both literal and figurative, and that when we trust in Him, we can experience His Peace even in the midst of life's most difficult challenges.

Philippians 4:4-9 -Paul's Letter to the Philippians

In this passage, Paul encourages the believers in Philippi to live in joy and Peace, even in the face of difficulty. He reminds them that the Peace of God, which surpasses all understanding, will guard their hearts and minds in Christ Jesus. This passage offers practical advice on how to live in the fullness of God's Peace through prayer, gratitude, and focusing on what is true, noble, and praiseworthy.

Isaiah 61-62 –The Spirit anoints us

The Spirit of the Lord brings healing, freedom, and joy. In His Kingdom of Peace, the broken are restored, the captives released, and all things made new. His people shine as a beacon of righteousness, clothed in salvation, walking in His Spirit. No longer forsaken, they are His delight, at peace with God and each other. The world will see His glory in them, as He establishes His everlasting Peace, His Kingdom, His Spirit, His people, all made new in Him.

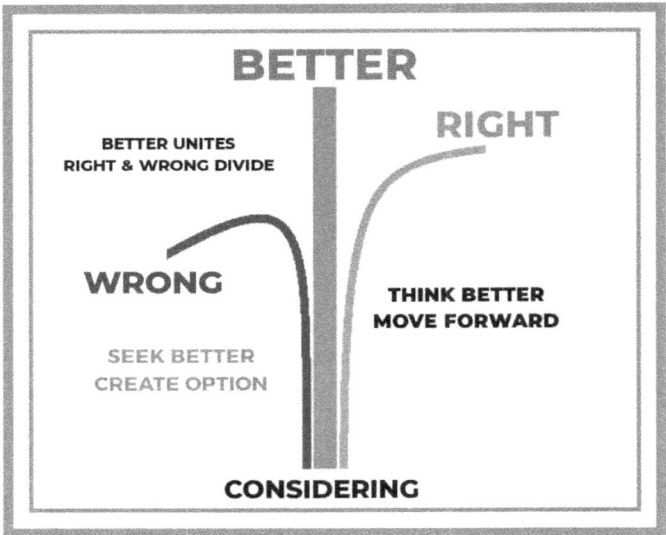

BETTER

RIGHT

**BETTER UNITES
RIGHT & WRONG DIVIDE**

WRONG

**THINK BETTER
MOVE FORWARD**

SEEK BETTER
CREATE OPTION

CONSIDERING

Seeking better creates opportunity by
delivering an option to right or wrong. We can
ask what's better rather than judge right from
wrong and come together in what's best for all.

Chapter 13

The Universal Call to the Gospel of Peace

Peace as a Universal Message For Everyone

Throughout the history of salvation, the message of Peace has been central to God's plan for humanity. From the prophecies of the Prince of Peace in Isaiah, to the angels proclaiming the mission of Jesus "Peace on Earth, goodwill to all" at Jesus' birth, to Christ Himself preaching Peace and reconciliation, the call to Peace is the heartbeat of the Gospel. Peace is heaven's name, the identity of God's Kingdom, and the very essence of Christ's mission on Earth.

The Gospel of Peace is not a message limited to a single group of people or a particular time in history. It is universal, calling all individuals, nations, races, tribes, and peoples to embrace His Spiritual Kingdom of Peace. In this chapter, we look at how the Gospel of Peace reaches beyond borders, cultures, and languages, offering hope, reconciliation, grace, and divine harmony to all who will receive it into their heart and conscience.

As followers of Christ, we are called not only to live in this Peace but also to enthusiastically spread it. The mission of the Great Commission is, at its heart, the spreading of the Gospel of Peace, inviting others into the fullness of life in Christ Jesus and into the Kingdom where His Peace reigns throughout all there is. Our mission is to extend this call to every corner of the world, proclaiming Jesus is our Peace because Jesus is Peace and Peace as heaven's name. Jesus in and amongst us brings heaven to Earth. Word to flesh, Peace into being. His Kingdom come, and will being done, already available to our hearts and minds, and within our conscience as well.

How the Gospel of Peace is Meant for All Humanity

The Gospel of Peace is God's invitation to all. Every person, tribe, group, and nation to participate in His Kingdom of Peace, as citizens and envoys here on Earth. Ephesians 2:17 says, "He came and preached Peace to you who were far away and Peace to those who were near." Jesus' message of Peace was never exclusive, it was meant for all, from the Jew to the Gentile, from the powerful to the marginalized, from those within the religious fold to those far outside.

The early Church, under the leadership of the apostles, was charged with the task of spreading this message of restoration and Peace to the ends of the Earth. In Acts 10:36, Peter proclaims, "You know the message God sent to the people of Israel, announcing the good news of Peace through Jesus Christ, who is Lord of all." This passage underscores the universality of the Gospel, Christ is Lord of all, and His Peace is for everyone.

In Christ, the barriers that divide humanity, whether they be cultural, social, racial, or political, are torn down. Ephesians 2:14 says, "For He Himself is our Peace, who has made the two groups one and has destroyed the barrier, the dividing wall of hostility." Jesus does not merely offer a temporary solution to humanity's conflict; He is Peace personified, bringing reconciliation between humanity and God, as well as between human beings.

The mission of the Church, therefore, is to bring this message of reconciliation and Peace to the world. We are diplomats and envoys of God's Kingdom, which is to say, Jesus' Kingdom of Peace, calling people to turn from the world's ways of war and conflict, violence, and division, and embrace His way of Peace instead.

Spreading the Good News of Jesus' Kingdom of Peace

Jesus' parting words to His disciples, known as the Great Commission in Matthew 28:19-20, were clear: "Go and make disciples of all nations, baptizing them in the name of the Father and of the Son and of the Holy Spirit, and teaching them to obey everything I have commanded you." This commission is, at its core, a call to spread the Gospel of Peace to everyone, everywhere, as well as all nations throughout Earth.

The Gospel of Peace is not merely an individual call to salvation; it is the proclamation of a Kingdom, His Kingdom, where Peace reigns supreme. Jesus invites us into His Kingdom, not as subjects of a distant ruler, but as children of God and fellow-citizens of Peace. Our task, as followers of Christ, is to bring this message of hope and Peace to a flawed and broken world, showing that the ways of violence, war, and division are not the ways of God at all.

His early Church members embraced this divine mission wholeheartedly. In the midst of persecution, political turmoil, and social upheaval, the apostles and early Christians spread the Gospel of Peace and grace across the

Roman Empire and beyond. They proclaimed that in Christ, God was reconciling the world to Himself, and that through Jesus, a new way of life, a way of Peace, was possible.

This call to spread the Gospel of Peace is as urgent today as it was back then. We live in a world deeply fractured by conflict, injustice, and division. Yet, the Gospel of Peace is the answer to the deepest longings of the human heart, a longing for wholeness, for unity, for healing, belonging, grace and reconnection.

As Christ's ambassadors, we are tasked with the privilege and responsibility of carrying this message of Peace to the ends of the Earth, proclaiming that Jesus is our Peace, and that His Kingdom is open to all who will come.

The Mission to Live Out the Golden Rule in All Nations

At the heart of Jesus' teaching on Peace is the Golden Rule for all, "So in all things whatsoever, in everything, do to others as you would have them fairly do to you" (Matthew 7:12). This simple yet profound teaching is the foundation for a life lived in Peace. The Golden Rule is not merely a moral guideline, Jesus called it the law and the prophets. It is a reflection of God's character and the nature of His Kingdom of Peace.

To live out the Golden Rule for all is to live in harmony and unity with God's will for Peace among our human endeavours, relationships, and community. In Ephesians 4:1-6, Pauls beseeches us that we walk worthy of the vocation wherewith we are called, with all lowliness and meekness, in our longsuffering, forbear one another in love.

Endeavouring to keep the unity of the Spirit in the bond of Peace. There is one body, and one Spirit, even as we are called in one hope of our calling. One Lord, one faith, one baptism, one God and Father of all, who is above all, and through all, and in you all."

In spreading the Gospel of Peace, we are also called to model this way of living in every interaction, whether within our own community or in our travels to other nations. The Golden Rule for all, transcends cultural boundaries and is a universal expression of God's desire for humanity, that we would treat one another with love, compassion, respect, and fairness.

As we share the Gospel of Peace, we must also live it out, by demonstrating the Peace we proclaim in our actions. Our lives should reflect the unity, calmness, harmony, kindness, and justice, that are characteristic of the Kingdom of Peace. In doing so, we not only invite others into God's Peace, but also become living witnesses to the transformative power of His Peace.

Peace as Heaven's Name: A Universal Message for the Ages

The call to spread the Gospel of Peace is not limited by time or place, it is a universal message for all the ages, reflecting the eternal nature of God's Kingdom. Peace is heaven's name, and it is the identity of the Kingdom of God. When we proclaim the Gospel, we are proclaiming heaven on earth, inviting humanity into the reality of Peace that has always been God's plan. Jesus in and amongst us brings His Peace into being.

As Isaiah 9:7 declares, "Of the greatness of His government and Peace there will be no end." The Kingdom of Peace is everlasting. It is the will of God performing it and the word of God that declares it so, and as we participate in the spreading of the good news of the Gospel, we are part of something far greater than ourselves. We are joining with the eternal mission of God to reconcile the world to Himself and to establish a Peace that will never end.

Practical Applications:

Remaining in Peace:

In your daily life, practice remaining in Peace by intentionally connecting with God's Spirit of Peace through scripture, prayer, reflection, and kindness to all you encounter. Reflect on how Peace is not just an internal feeling but a relationship with Christ, who is Peace incarnate. Stay mindful of how God's Peace reigns over every part of your life, even in times of difficulty, chaos, or stress. 2 Thessalonians 3:16 "Now the Lord of Peace himself give you peace always by all means. The Lord be with us all"

Living in Peace

Living in Peace means embodying the message of the Gospel of Peace in your interactions with others. Treat others with respect, kindness, patience, love, and even when faced with struggle, remember that respect is an act of equality. When disagreements or conflict arise, ask yourself how you can reflect the Golden Rule for all in your actions and words. Living in Peace is all about being an example of Christ's love restoring the world around you.

Walking with His Peace:

Walking with His Peace means becoming an His special envoy and ambassador of the Gospel of Peace, spreading Christ's message to others not just through words, but through your actions. Be a living testimony to the transformative power of Peace, sharing Jesus' Kingdom of Peace wherever you go. As Ephesians 6:15 says, "And with your feet fitted with the readiness that comes from the gospel of Peace," be prepared to carry this message with you into every encounter and situation.

Group Study Questions

1. Joke: What does an old eraser and Jesus have in common? Both died to take our mistakes away.
2. What does it mean for the Gospel of Peace to be a universal message? How does this change the way we think about the mission of the Church?
3. Joke: Why can't Jesus work in a kitchen? Because of cross contamination.
4. In what ways does Jesus serve as both Peace personified and the King of Peace?
5. How does the Gospel of Peace speak to the deepest needs of our world today?

Up Next:

In concluding this chapter, we've explored how the Gospel of Peace is a universal message, a call for all of humanity to join with Jesus in His Kingdom of Peace. This message is urgent and transformative, and we, as followers of Christ, are called and privileged to carry it to the ends of the Earth.

In Chapter 14: Peace is at Hand, we will delve into the prophetic declaration Jesus is coming soon, and that His Kingdom of Peace is about to be fully revealed. We will examine what it means to live in expectation of His return, and how we can prepare our hearts for the coming reign of Peace.

Recommended Bible Reading:

Luke 10:1-12 Jesus Sends Out Seventy-Two

In this passage, Jesus sends out seventy-two of His followers to proclaim the coming of the Kingdom of

God. He instructs them to offer Peace to every household they enter, to heal the sick, and proclaim that the Kingdom of God and His Peace are near in coming. This story highlights the mission of Peace and the urgency of spreading the Gospel of Peace to all who are willing to receive it.

Acts 10:34-48 –The Conversion of Cornelius

This account of the conversion of Cornelius, a Roman centurion, illustrates the universal call of the Gospel of Peace. Peter's vision and subsequent visit to the household of Cornelius shows that the message of Christ is not limited to the Jewish people, but is intended for all nations. Cornelius and his household receive the Holy Spirit, demonstrating the Gospel of Peace transcends cultural and ethnic boundaries.

Isaiah 26:3-4 -God's perfect PEACE

Perfect PEACE belongs to those who trust in the Lord, whose minds are stayed on Him. Not the fleeting calm of the world, but a peace rooted in the everlasting Rock. He is unshaken, faithful, and true. Trust in Him forever, for His strength upholds, His love secures, and in Him, all fear fades. His peace is the steady hand guiding us through every storm.

Ephesians 2:4-9 –His Grace lifts us up

Rich in mercy, God made us alive in Christ, saved by grace, not by works. We were lost, but now raised with Him, seated in heavenly places. His gift is free, no striving, no earning—only receiving. Grace flows through faith, a love beyond measure. No one can boast, for salvation is His alone, a masterpiece of mercy, unfolding in eternity.

Chapter 14

Peace is at Hand

The Prophetic Declaration of Jesus' Coming

As we near the conclusion of this journey, we turn our attention once again to the final fulfilment of the Gospel of Peace, the imminent return of Jesus Christ, the King of Peace. Throughout the Scriptures, we see that Jesus' coming is not only a promise of salvation but also the ultimate performing and perfecting of His Kingdom of Peace. His return will usher in an era of universal Peace, where all things will be reconciled under His rule, and the brokenness of the world will be healed forevermore.

Peace is at hand, and Jesus, as the Prince of Peace crowned King, is coming soon to bring heaven's Peace to earth in the fullness of God's Glory. This is a time of hope, preparation, and invitation, a call to live in expectation of His return, embracing the Peace of Christ in the here and now as a foretaste of the eternal Peace that is to come.

Peace is at hand, history is about to change, the body of Christ and the entire world is about to discover Peace as the name of Jesus' kingdom and adopt Peace as heaven's name. The good news of Peace will significantly change all things, and all things will be new again. This will be a profound coming of Christ, however still we'll need to wait for the day of perfection when finally, we get to shake Jesus' hand, look into His eyes, and say thanks for all He has done.

The Failure of Peace by Superior Firepower and the Call to Believe in Peace

Throughout history, humanity has often sought to achieve Peace through superior firepower, through violence, domination, and control. The philosophy of "Peace through strength and training for war" has been a guiding principle for empires, nations, and governments, all believing that force can bring about stability and harmony. Yet, as we have explored in earlier chapters, this approach has consistently failed to deliver true, everlasting Peace. Instead, it has perpetuated cycles of retaliation, violence, and harm.

Genesis 6:11 tells of God's distaste for violence. Even destroying the world because of it. In Matthew 26:52, Jesus says that all who draw the sword will die by the sword. This powerful statement is a timely reminder violence only begets violence, and true lasting Peace can never be forged through force. The Kingdom of Peace operates on a different principle, the principle of Peace through love, grace, mateship, forgiveness, kindness, care, and eternal reconnection.

As we await the return of Jesus, we are called to reject the false promise of peace by superior firepower and to embrace the true Peace that comes from Christ Jesus alone, unifying us in Spirit. The world's system of deterring war through violence is temporal and doomed to fail, but the Kingdom of Peace that Jesus brings is eternal and delivers complete restoration.

The failure of "peace by superior firepower" is not just a

political or military issue, it is a spiritual issue. At the heart of this philosophy lies the belief that human strength can solve the problems of the world, and can achieve a lasting peace through our own efforts. But impossible while we trust in the gun more than God. Jesus calls us to surrender our reliance on force and to trust in His divine Peace, (John 16:33) "These things I have spoken unto you, that in me ye might have Peace. In the world ye shall have tribulation: but be of good cheer; I have overcome the world." Rejoice.

The Coming Reign of Jesus' Kingdom of Peace

The return of Jesus is not merely an end to the present age; it is the beginning of His eternal reign of the Kingdom of Peace. In Revelation 21:3-4, we are given a vision of what this Kingdom will look like: "And I heard a loud voice from the throne saying, 'Look! God's dwelling place is now among the people, and He will dwell with them. They will be His people, and God Himself will be with them and be their God. He will wipe every tear from their eyes. There will be no more death or mourning or crying or pain, for the old order of things has passed away."

This is the fulfilment of the promise of Peace. In the Kingdom of Peace, all the sorrows, conflicts, and brokenness of the world will be healed. Violence will cease, and the weapons of war will be transformed into tools of creation and life. As the prophet Isaiah foretold Isaiah 43:16-19, "Thus saith the LORD, which maketh a way in the sea, and a path in the mighty waters; which bringeth forth the chariot and horse, the army and the power; they shall lie down together, they shall not rise: they are extinct, they are quenched as tow. Remember ye not the former things, neither consider the things of old. Behold, I will do a new thing; now it shall spring forth; shall ye not know it? I will even make a way in the wilderness, and rivers in the desert."

Jesus, as the King of Peace, will reign with justice and righteousness. His Kingdom will be one of healing and restoration, where the divisions that separate humanity, whether they be racial, social, or economic, will be erased, and all people will live in harmony united under His rule and umbrella of grace. The Kingdom of Peace is not just a future hope; it's an ultimate reality God has promised, we can live now.

An Invitation to Embrace Peace and Kindness as the True Path Forward

As we stand on the threshold of the awakening to the Kingdom of Peace, we are faced with a choice to continue living by the world's systems of force, conflict, and self-reliance, or to embrace the Peace of Christ and eternal way of kindness.

Do we face the world as warriors or see all peoples as mates? Jesus invites us to choose the path of Peace, to live in the Spirit of His Kingdom come, and to be His agents of change in a world desperate for healing.

Kindness is Peace in action. Every act of compassion, every moment of forgiveness, every effort to bridge the divides, is a reflection of His Kingdom of Peace. As we live out His Gospel of Peace, we are not only preparing ourselves for the coming reign of Christ, but also bringing glimpses of His Reign into the present.

Romans 16:20, "And the God of peace shall bruise Satan under your feet shortly. The grace of our Lord Jesus Christ be with you. Amen."

Here lies an invitation to live in the fullness of His Peace now, even as we await its complete fulfilment at His return. By embracing Jesus as Peace, we reject the ways of the world and align ourselves with the eternal Kingdom that is already breaking through.

Jesus as Peace, and Our Role in Living Out His Peace

As we have explored throughout this book, Peace is not just a moment, feeling, sensation, or abstract concept, it is the very identity of God's Kingdom. Peace is heaven's name, the essence of Christ's mission, and the ultimate reality toward which all of creation is moving. Jesus is Peace, and in Him, we find our true identity, purpose, and calling.

Our role, as followers of Jesus, is to live at peace, in Peace, with His Peace in every aspect of our lives. This means embodying the values of the Kingdom and Spirit of God, in our daily interactions with the world in general. It means being living temples of Peace, proclaiming the good news Jesus is coming soon and His reign of Peace will transform everything there is.

The Saints Cry: Come, Jesus, Come

In the final words of Revelation, we hear the cry of the saints: "Amen. Come, Lord Jesus, come!" (Revelation 22:20). This is the cry of all who long for the fullness of Peace to be revealed, for the return of the King and for the completion of His eternal perfected Kingdom. As we live in anticipation of His return, let this cry be on our lips and in our hearts: "Come, Jesus, come."

Peace is at hand. There comes a time soon when all will know the name of Jesus' kingdom. When all will know Peace as heaven's name. And we will see through a fresh set of eyes and be seen in a new day light. History's course will be realigned and humanity will leave behind the violence of the past. So eagerly we await the coming of Jesus' Kingdom of Peace. Called to play our part in the reformation of the Gospel of Peace and prepare the way, living in His Peace, proclaiming to the world, Peace is at hand, come Jesus come.

Practical Applications:

Remaining in Peace:

To remain in Peace, focus on the imminent return of Christ and the Kingdom of Peace He is bringing. Even in times of uncertainty, know that Peace is at hand. Daily prayer and meditation on scriptures such as Ezekiel 37:26; "Moreover I will make a Covenant of Peace with them; it shall be an everlasting covenant and I will place them, and multiply them, and will set my sanctuary in the midst of them for evermore." Hold onto this promise and let it guard your heart from fear and anxiety.

Living in Peace:

Living in Peace means actively rejecting the world's methods of achieving Peace through force, superior firepower, or domination. Instead, choose empathy, kindness, compassion, forgiveness, and fun, in every interaction. Let your life be a witness to the Kingdom of Peace, and when conflicts arise, seek resolution through restoration, grace, truth, and love, following the example of Jesus Christ, King of Peace.

Remember Abraham paid tribute to the King of Peace and better when we do. Hebrews 7:1-3, "For this Melchisedec, King of Salem, priest of the most high God, who met Abraham returning from the slaughter of the kings, and blessed him; To whom also Abraham gave a tenth part of all; first being by interpretation King of righteousness, and after that also King of Salem, which is, King of Peace; Without father, without mother, without descent, having neither the beginning of days, nor end of life; but made like unto the Son of God; abides a priest continually."

Walking with His Peace:

Walking with His Peace means embodying the mission of Peace as you await the return of the King of Peace. Let your actions be guided by the principles of the Kingdom of God, living as an advocate of the Gospel of Peace. Share the message of Christ's coming reign with others, have a laugh, and be a Peacemaker in your relationships, your community, and the wider world in general.

Romans 10:15, "And how shall they preach, except they be sent? as it is written, How beautiful are the feet of them that preach the gospel of Peace, and bring glad tidings of good things!" Be ready to share His Peace with all, wherever you may go.

Group Study Questions

1. How does the return of Jesus fulfil the promise of Peace and bring about the Kingdom?
2. What are the dangers of relying on the philosophy of "Peace by superior firepower," and how does Jesus' message challenge that approach?
3. How can we embrace kindness and Peace in our daily lives as a way of preparing for the return of Christ?
4. What does the return of Jesus mean to you?
5. Joke: What sport did Jesus play? Lacrosse.

Recommended Bible Reading:

Isaiah 9:6-8 —The Prophecy of the Prince of Peace

This passage prophesies the coming of the God of Peace, whose government and Peace will have no end, and how it is God's will performing it. It highlights the eternal nature of Christ's reign and the Kingdom of Peace He is perfecting.

Revelation 21:1-7 —The New Heaven and the New Earth

This passage gives us a vision of the new heaven and new earth where God will dwell with His people, and there will be no more pain, suffering, or death. It paints a picture of the eternal Kingdom of Peace, where all things are made new, and the fullness of God's Peace is realized for all of creation

Matthew 6:31-34 —His Kingdom is near

Do not worry about tomorrow, for His Kingdom is near. Seek first His righteousness, and all will be added. The world chases after fleeting things, but the Father knows what you need. His Kingdom is not of lack but abundance, not fear but trust. In Him, provision flows, burdens lift, and each day is covered in divine care, ruled by love.

Chapter 15

Reflecting on Learning War No More

Peace by Jesus Christ: Learning War No More

Peace by Jesus Christ: Learning War No More presents a compelling, transformative vision of Peace not just as a virtue, but the very identity of God's Kingdom, heaven's name, and Spirit of Truth. The book reveals how adopting Jesus as Peace invites humanity to transcend violent behaviours and embrace a divine order where Peace reigns supreme.

In John 20:27, Jesus invites Thomas into His presence to taste and see, to experience His miraculous Peace for himself. Thomas did, and responded, "My Lord, my God."

My book offered to take you on a journey through a biblical revelation of the good news of Jesus' kingdom of Peace, beginning with Melchizedek and Abram paying tribute to the king of Peace (Genesis 14:18-20) and the nature of Jesus Christ as the Prince of Peace, continuing through the failures of "peace by superior firepower," and leading to the coming reign of Christ's Kingdom of Peace.

A wild ride through the scriptures when taken on board and taken to heart. Peace by Jesus Christ calls individuals, communities, and nations to reject the world's violent solutions and to live in the fullness of God's Peace, both now and into all eternity.

Top Five Arguments for Adopting Jesus as Peace

1. Jesus is Peace: The Word Becoming Flesh

At the heart of my book is the central truth Jesus is Peace incarnate. When the Word became flesh, Jesus brought heaven's Peace to earth, making it accessible and tangible for all humanity.

The overwhelming scriptural evidence Peace is core to God's Message, supported by the Spirit of Truth being available to everyone, men, women, and children everywhere, points to God's desire to establish further His Peace on Earth, Goodwill to all Humanity.

Luke 2:24 tells us the mission statement of Jesus proclaimed by the angels at Jesus' birth. The eternal endeavour of us all. In this we march on in the complexities between "it is done" and yet, "we are still building," the tension between the "already" and the "not yet." John 1:14 tells us that the Word became flesh and made His dwelling among us. Jesus within, means bringing Peace into Being, as we live in light of His grace, forgiveness, truth, and divine miraculous Peace.

Isaiah 9:6 calls Jesus the Prince of Peace, and throughout His ministry, He embodied and preached Peace, near and far, healing the broken, welcoming the marginalised, and showing us how to live at peace, in Peace with His Peace.

2. Peace, the Spirit of Truth, and the Kingdom of God

Peace is not just a personal state; it is the very essence of the Holy Spirit and the hallmark of the Kingdom of God. Peace is Heaven's Name, The Order of God's Reign. In my book, we explored how living in Peace means walking in the Spirit, divinely guided by the Spirit of Truth.

In Galatians 5:22-23, Peace is one of the fruits of the Spirit, reminding us that to truly live in the Kingdom of Peace, we must cultivate these fruits in our lives. Jesus' teachings, especially the Golden Rule for all in Matthew 7:12, reflect this spirit of Peace, calling us to treat others with the same kindness, grace, love, and respect that we desire for ourselves.

3. Jesus in and Amongst Us Brings Peace to Earth

The message of this book is Peace is heaven's name and Jesus in and amongst us brings Peace to earth. Jesus' presence, both in His earthly ministry and through the Holy Spirit within us, allows us to experience His Peace in the here and now. John 14:27 reminds us that Jesus leaves us His Peace, a Peace unlike anything the world can offer.

Colossians 3:15 calls us in Peace, to let the Peace of Christ rule in our hearts, showing that by living in His Peace, we become vessels of Peace in the world. Through Jesus' Peace, we are reconciled with God, and through His example, we are called to be agents of reconciliation and healing in a divided and violent world, enthusiastically sharing the gospel of Peace in word and deed.

4. The Failure of Peace by Superior Firepower

One of the most powerful arguments in the book is the void caused in not preaching Peace by Jesus Christ filled by the world's brutal philosophy of "peace by superior firepower" which is continuing to bring people harm to this very day. History is full and overflowing with examples of how the reliance on violence, force, and domination has only led to more conflict and suffering. Matthew 26:52 teaches those who live by the sword will die by the sword, pointing to the futility of seeking Peace through violence.

Instead, my book urged readers to adopt the way of Jesus, where Peace is achieved through love, forgiveness, and self-sacrifice. The Kingdom of God, Peace, operates on a completely different wave-length to conventional thinking and understanding, meaning that Peace comes through reconciliation, not force. Mates at Peace, not warriors, willing to go to war.

5. The Coming Reign of the Kingdom of Peace

The final chapters focus on the prophetic vision of Jesus' return and the establishment of His Perfected Kingdom of Peace. Revelation 21:1-4 describes the ultimate new heaven and new earth, where death, sorrow, and pain are no more, and God's perfect Peace reigns throughout. In this perfected Kingdom, the divisions that have plagued humanity since the beginning will be healed, and Jesus' Peace will cover the earth as the waters make up the sea.

My book concludes with the invitation to prepare for this Kingdom of Peace by living in His Peace now, embodying Jesus' teachings, and spreading the Gospel of Peace to all nations. Micah prophesies a time when nations will beat their swords into ploughshares and learn war no more, a vision this book holds as an ultimate goal.

Chapter 16

Conclusion:

Peace by Jesus Christ is a word-based vision of humanity transcending violent behaviour. We can discover Peace and learn war no more.

Peace is heaven's name.

There comes a time when every Christian will want to learn the name of Jesus' kingdom. A time when all will know the name of His kingdom. When all will know Peace as heaven's name. And we will see through a fresh set of eyes and be seen in a new day light.

History missing the name of Christ's kingdom has left humanity at the mercy of a brutal philosophy and way, reaching all the way back to the Stone-Age and stereo-typical cave man, which epitomises, 'peace by superior firepower.'

History's failure to recognize the name of Jesus' Kingdom as Peace has exacted a heavy toll on humanity. This void, created by ignoring the way of Peace, has left generations reliant on brutality, force, violence, and cruelty as a means to impose their own will over others. Instead of embracing the belief in Peace that Jesus offers, humanity has placed its faith in dominance and force, perpetuating cycles of harm and division. The cost of this void is felt most deeply by those who are vulnerable, women, children, and the broken among us.

The weight of prejudice, violence, and discrimination against them is a stark reminder of what happens when the spirit of Peace is absent. The pain endured by the oppressed and marginalized is a call for humanity to turn away from these patterns of harm and embrace the grace, healing and reconciliation found in the Kingdom of Peace.

The violent way we currently uphold peace is costing us our planet and threatening our very way of life. All of creation is longing for the day our world is determined by Peace, rather than destined to destruction by the devastating effects self-serving, self-centred selfishness has had upon us, our way, our world, and our ideas.

It is our truths that shape our behaviours. What we believe determines our actions, words, and reflections. New truths can reshape our behaviour. What we believe to be true determines what we will do, how we will act, what we will say, and what we will reflect upon. What many believe, many will do and many become. Many can be one in endeavour.

Peace welcomes all.

Jesus reigns over a kingdom named Peace. We can abandon war and brutality and embrace His truths that liberate us from yesterday's ways of violence and force. Jesus gives us an option to believe in His Peace instead. Rather than fighting each other, or trying to harm someone in order to teach them a lesson, we can confront self-serving attitudes like vanity, greed, discrimination, dominance, hypocrisy, and violence.

By prioritizing conscience over ego, we can embody His Peace and extend our goodwill forgiving more readily, and learning better not to take offence at all. Primarily, Peace by Jesus Christ, is Peace in the golden rule for all. In doing this, we nurture a community of profound peace, in Peace along with His Peace, bringing heaven to earth through Jesus Christ, who is our ultimate complete PEACE abiding in and amongst us all.

It is a shortcoming that more people would know the name of a football team than could quote you the name of Jesus' kingdom. I hope my book can help in addressing this shortcoming because I want that to change. I want everyone, everywhere, to know of the good news of Jesus' kingdom of Peace. Peace is at hand and the world will be changed in its learning of it. So now when reading scripture, we find the term peace can often be better interpreted, as Peace, or even PEACE, or even Jesus.

Jesus is Peace. Peace is more than a moment, more than a feeling or absence of war or chaos. Peace is more than a place. Peace is an endeavour. An encounter. We experience Peace. Jesus is our Peace. Jesus embodies PEACE. We embody Jesus through the Holy Ghost. Jesus is PERFECT PEACE. Peace is heaven's name. Jesus in and amongst us brings heaven to Earth. Peace manifests, as word becomes flesh. Peace into being.

Peace is by faith, not by force.

Peace is a blessing and can unite people on a grand scale in Spirit, brand, belonging, purpose, and pursuit. His kingdom come, and His will being done, Peace and goodwill to all. Peace delivers identity. Peace is transformative. Many can be one in Peace. Peace comforts our soul, tames our ego, renews our mind, refreshes our emotions, and revives our will and way.

Kindness is Peace in action. Peace is the workings of love resulting in Joy. Peace reproves our view of sin with grace, our righteousness in faith of a better hope, and judgement by salvation of new truths, where Holy Spirit coaching replaces the punishment, we deserve. Now, because of Christ we can hear directly from God Himself. Peace by Jesus Christ is by faith, whereas a peace by a superior firepower is by force, coercion, control, and containment.

Noah's story is faith over violence. The significance of God's kingdom of Peace, is Jesus' abiding in us and amongst us, and the freedom from harm this can bring. We become living temples of Peace, pouring out grace from above, developing better, how to deal with offence and finding new ways to be kind. Breaking free from past ravages of vanity, greed, prejudice, violence, hypocrisy, and dominance.

Healed in Peace, grace, truth, kindness, and fun. Living epistles of Peace active in a golden age under the Golden Rule, learning and training for war no more, where we live life unto Life by grace, and not unto death by law. Kindness is a strength, not a weakness. Violence is a weakness, not a strength. Education is better than imposed by force. Persuasion is better than invasion. Friendships are better than battleships. Help is better than harm.

Overcome our ego, overcome violent behaviour

We can become living Peace journals sharing the wonder and privilege of being human in the presence of God, in His equal opportunity world for all. Saints becoming temples. All having access to God's leading into all kindness and truth, which is to say, His love.

Simply by asking God to be our conscience for us we become more conscience conscious, more spiritually aware, even

Spirit-Guided in our Saviour, Jesus Christ. We can overcome our ego and live in Peace, peaceably, united as one diversity together.

We can learn to be at peace, in Peace, with His Peace, and extend our Peace beyond each other unto all, including our planet as well.

Peace can be our perfected identity and our inevitable eternal destination as well, when adopting Peace as heaven's name. Peace presents a realistic word-based vision to excite humanity and inspire people to push on, and further lean into transcending violent behaviour, turning from force to care, as we remember God is not a big fan of violence as Genesis 6:13 would suggest, "And God said unto Noah, The end of all flesh is come before me; for the earth is filled with violence through them; and, behold, I will destroy them with the earth."

Jesus is our Peace

Peace as heaven's name enhances the name above all names Jesus Christ and is no challenge against Him. Indeed, Peace is a word magnified. Psalm 138:2, I will worship toward thy holy temple, and praise thy name for thy loving kindness and for thy truth: for thou hast magnified thy word above all thy name.

Peace be with you.

Prayer for Peace

Peace on Earth
and Goodwill to All Mankind

Heavenly Father,

Lord of all creation, the God of Peace, we come before You with grateful hearts, humbled by Your love and the gift of Your Son, Jesus Christ, who is our Prince of Peace. We thank You for the Gospel of Peace that invites us into Your Kingdom, a Kingdom not ruled by force or violence, but by grace, forgiveness, and love.

We stand in awe of Your eternal Peace, a Peace that transcends all understanding, that calms the storms within us and in the world around us. We thank You for sending the Holy Spirit, the Spirit of Truth, to dwell within us and guide us in the ways of Your Everlasting Kingdom of Peace.

Lord, we pray for Peace on Earth, for the world You so lovingly created. As we await the return of Jesus Christ, the King of Peace, we ask that Your Peace would reign in our hearts, our homes, schools, workplaces, our communities, tribes, and our nations. May Your Peace flow through us, healing broken relationships, mending divisions, and restoring unity among all people.

Forgive us, Lord, for the times we have failed to walk in Your ways. Help us to reject the false promise of "Peace by superior firepower" and instead embrace Your way of Peace, following the example of Your dear Son Christ Jesus, who showed us how to live in love, kindness, and humility.

Father God, we ask for Your guidance as we live as ambassadors of Your Peace in a world desperate for reconciliation. Fill us with the courage to be Peacemakers, to embody the Golden Rule for all, and to treat others as we would want to be treated. Help us to be agents of reconciliation, sharing the Gospel of Peace with all nations, so that the world may know the fullness of Your love.

We pray for the healing of wounds caused by conflict, injustice, and oppression. Lord, we long for the day when You return and reign over Your Eternal Peace, which will be fully established in the reconciling of all things.

Until that day, strengthen us to live in Your Peace daily, to walk with Your Peace in every step we take, and to shine as lights in the darkness, proclaiming the good news that Peace is at hand.

We join with the saints in crying out, "Come, Lord Jesus, come." Bring forth Your Kingdom of Peace, and may Your goodwill toward all mankind be seen in the lives of those who serve You. Unite us as one people under the banner of Your Peace and lead us into the divine joy of Your presence.

Lord, hallowed be your name, your kingdom come and your will be done, on earth as it is in heaven. Give us this day our daily bread and forgive us our trespasses as we forgive them that trespass against us, and lead us not into temptation but deliver us from evil, for thine is the kingdom, the power, and the glory now and for ever and evermore. You alone are Lord God Almighty, creator of all that there is. We thank you for being our Lord, LORD.

This we pray in your name, Lord. In the name above all names, Jesus Christ, King of Peace.

Amen

Appendix

Scripture Pointing to Peace
as heaven's name. Jesus as Peace.

Micah 4:3, And he shall judge among many people, and rebuke strong nations afar off; and they shall beat their swords into ploughshares, and their spears into pruninghooks: nation shall not lift up a sword against nation, neither shall they learn war any more.

Matthew 11:28-30, Come unto me, all ye that labour and are heavy laden, and I will give you rest. Take my yoke upon you, and learn of me; for I am meek and lowly in heart: and ye shall find rest unto your souls. For my yoke is easy, and my burden is light.

Colossians 1:12-14, Giving thanks unto the Father, which hath made us meet (qualified) to be partakers of the inheritance of the saints in light: Who hath delivered us from the power of darkness, and hath translated us into the kingdom of his dear Son: In whom we have redemption through his blood, even the forgiveness of sins:

Matthew 7:12, Therefore all things whatsoever ye would that men should do to you, do ye even so to them: for this is the law and the prophets.

John 18:37, ...Every one that is of the truth heareth my voice.

Gift of Peace:

John 14:27, *Peace I leave with you, my Peace I give unto you: not as the world giveth, give I unto you. Let not your heart be troubled, neither let it be afraid.*

Call to Peace

Colossians 3:15, *... Since members of one body called to Peace, giving thanks for our peace.*

Living in Peace:

2 Corinthians 13:11, *Finally, brethren, farewell. Be perfect, be of good comfort, be of one mind, live in PEACE; and the God of Peace and love shall be with you.*

Focus of Peace:

Romans 8:6, *For to be carnally minded is death; but to be spiritually minded is life and PEACE.*

Path of Peace:

Psalms 34:13-14, *Keep thy tongue from evil, and lips from speaking guile. Depart from evil, and do good; seek PEACE, and pursue it.*

Author of Peace:

1 Corinthians 14:33, *For God is not the author of confusion, but of PEACE, as in all churches of the saints.*

God of Peace:

Romans 15:33, *Now the God of Peace be with you all. Amen.*

Wisdom of Peace:

Proverbs 3:17, *Her ways are ways of pleasantness, and all her paths are PEACE.*

Way of Peace:

Luke 1:79, *To give light to them that sit in darkness and in the shadow of death, to guide our feet into the way of PEACE.*

God's Will of Peace:

Jeremiah 29:11, *For I know the thoughts that I think toward you, saith the LORD, thoughts of PEACE, and not of evil, to give you an expected end.*

Message of Peace:

Acts 10:36, *The word which God sent unto the children of Israel, preaching PEACE by Jesus Christ: (he is Lord of all)*

Meaning of Peace:

Ephesians 4:3, *Endeavouring to keep the unity of the Spirit in the bond of PEACE.*

Mission of Peace:

Luke 2:14, *Glory to God in the highest, and on earth PEACE, good will toward men.*

Outlook of Peace:

Ephesians 6:15, *And your feet shod with the preparation of the gospel of PEACE;*

Heart of Peace:

Colossians 3:15, *And let the PEACE of God rule in your hearts, to the which also ye are called in one body; and be ye thankful.*

Power of Peace:

Ephesians 2:14, *Jesus is our PEACE ...*

Security of Peace:

Isaiah 26:3, *The LORD gives perfect PEACE to those whose faith is firm.*

Protection of Peace:

Philippians 4:7, *And the PEACE of God, which passeth all understanding, shall keep your hearts and minds through Christ Jesus.*

Direction of Peace:

Psalm 37:37, *Mark the perfect man, and behold the upright: for the end of that man is Peace.*

Significance of Peace:

Genesis 6:11, *And God said unto Noah, The end of all flesh is come before me, for the earth is filled with violence through them and behold I will destroy them with the earth.*

Importance of Peace:

Jesus within us. *We represent PEACE on Earth. Living life unto Life, and not unto death. (Rev.12:10-11)*

Experience of Peace:

John 16:33, *These things I have spoken unto you, that in me ye might have PEACE. In the world ye shall have tribulation: but be of good cheer; I have overcome the world.*

Lord of Peace:

2 Thessalonians 3:16, *Now the Lord of Peace himself give you PEACE always by all means. The Lord be with you all.*

King of Peace:

Hebrews 7:2, *To whom also Abraham gave a tenth part of all; first being by interpretation King of righteousness, and after that also King of Salem, which is (also) King of PEACE.*

Spirit of Peace:

John 14:27, *Peace I leave with you, my PEACE I give unto you: not as the world giveth, give I unto you. Let not your heart be troubled, neither let it be afraid.*

Covenant of Peace:

Ezekiel 37:26, *Moreover I will make a Covenant of*

PEACE with them; it shall be an everlasting covenant with them: and I will place them, and multiply them, and will set my sanctuary in the midst of them forevermore.

Kingdom of Peace:

Isaiah 9:7, *Of the increase of his government and PEACE there shall be no end, upon the throne of David, and upon his kingdom, to order it, and to establish it with judgment and with justice from henceforth even forever. The zeal of the LORD of hosts will perform this.*

Fellow citizens of Peace:

Ephesians 2:14-19, *For He is our Peace, who hath made both one, and hath broken down the middle wall of partition between us; Having abolished in his flesh the enmity, even the law of commandments contained in ordinances; for to make in himself of twain one new man, so making peace; And that he might reconcile both unto God in one body by the cross, having slain the enmity thereby: And came and preached PEACE to you which were afar off, and to them that were nigh. For through him we both have access by one Spirit unto the Father. Now therefore ye are no more strangers and foreigners, but Fellow citizens with the saints, and of the household.*

Victory of Peace:

Romans 16:20, *The God of Peace will soon crush Satan under your feet. The grace of our Lord Jesus be with you.*

Found in Peace:

2 Peter 3:14, *Wherefore, beloved, seeing that ye look for such things, be diligent that ye may be found of Him in Peace, without spot, and blameless.*

Glory of Peace:

Psalms 119:16, *Great PEACE have they which love thy law: and nothing shall offend them.*

Gospel of Peace:

Romans 10:15, *And how shall they preach, except they be sent? As it is written, How beautiful are the feet of them that preach the Gospel of PEACE, and bring glad tidings of good things!*

Blessing of Peace:

Numbers 6:24-26, *The LORD bless thee, and keep thee: The LORD make his face shine upon thee, and be gracious unto thee: The LORD lift up his countenance upon thee, and give thee PEACE.*

Jesus' Blessing of Peace:

Luke 24:36, *And as they thus spake, Jesus himself stood in the midst of them, and saith unto them, Peace be unto you.*

Acknowledgement

Citizens of Peace Media, COPMEDIA,

Acknowledges First Australians as the Traditional Owners and Custodians of this land and pays respect to Elders – past and present – and through them to all Aboriginal and Torres Strait Islander peoples.